RACE & EQUITY IN HIGHER EDUCATION

Proceedings and Papers of the ACE-Aspen Institute Seminar on Desegregation in Higher Education

Edited by Reginald Wilson

AMERICAN COUNCIL ON EDUCATION

Washington, D. C.

One Dupont Circle, Washington, D.C. 20036

Library of Congress Cataloging in Publication Data

ACE—Aspen Institute Seminar on Desegregation in Higher
Education (1981: Wye Plantation)
Race and equity in higher education.

1. College integration—United States—Congresses.
2. Educational equalization—United States—Congresses.
I. Wilson, Reginald. II. American Council on Education.
III. Aspen Institute for Humanistic Studies. IV. Title.
LC214.2.A33 1982 370.19′342 82-18459

ISBN 0-8268-1472-7

9 8 7 6 5 4 3 2 1

Printed in the United States of America

Contents

Foreword v

Preface vii

1. Race and Equity in Higher Education 1
   John Egerton

2. Demographics of Desegregation 28
   James E. Blackwell

3. A Political Taxonomy of Desegregation 71
   Jewel L. Prestage

4. Constitutional Requirements 104
   Paul R. Dimond

5. Toward Desegregation and Enhancement 138
   Albert H. Berrian

ACE-ASPEN INSTITUTE SEMINAR ON THE DESEGREGATION OF HIGHER EDUCATION

November 12-14, 1981 – Wye Plantation

PARTICIPANTS

Discussants:

Jean Fairfax, NAACP Legal Defense and Educational Fund, Inc.
Winfred Godwin, Southern Regional Education Board
Frank Keppel, Aspen Institute for Humanistic Studies
Harold Howe, II, Formerly Education VP, Ford Foundation
Eldridge McMillan, Southern Education Foundation
Samuel Myers, Executive Director, NAFEO
Charles Lyons, Fayetteville State University
J. W. Peltason, President, American Council on Education
Nathaniel Douglass, Office of Civil Rights
David Tatel, Hogan & Hartson, Former Director, Office of Civil Rights
Clarence Thomas, Director, Office of Civil Rights, Department of Education
John Toll, President, University of Maryland
John W. T. Webb, Regent, State of Maryland
J. Wade Gilley, Secretary of Education, Commonwealth of Virginia
Kenneth Tollett, Director, Institute for Study of Educational Policy
Luna Mishoe, President, Delaware State College
Harold Delaney, Executive Vice President, American Association of State Colleges and Universities

Authors:

Professor James Blackwell, University of Massachusetts, Boston
Professor Paul Dimond, University of Michigan (currently American University)
Professor Jewel Prestage, Southern University
Dr. Albert Berrian, President, Institute for Services to Education
Mr. Henry E. Cobb, Professor of History, Southern University, Baton Rouge

Observers:

Jay Heubert, Attorney, Litigation Division, Department of Justice
Ms. Claire Guthrie, Assistant Counsel, American Council on Education
Lorenzo Middleton, Chronicle of Higher Education

Staff:

John Egerton, Rapporteur
Leonard L. Haynes, III, Office for the Advancement of Public Negro Colleges
Reginald Wilson, Director, Office of Minority Concerns, ACE
James R. Jordan, Program Advisor, ACE

Foreword

Racial desegregation has been a matter of periodic and continuing interest in American higher education for the past half-century; since the mid-1960s, it has been a subject of particularly intense concern. As black Americans and other minorities have sought to overturn and overcome the legacy of segregation, questions of race and equity have assumed greater importance and urgency on virtually every college and university campus in the nation. Much change has taken place in the past decade, but many unresolved issues remain.

In the fall of 1981, the American Council on Education and the Aspen Institute for Humanistic Studies jointly sponsored a seminar on the desegregation of higher education. For three days in November, a small group of academicians and administrators, attorneys, government officials, and association executives met at the Aspen Institute's Wye Plantation conference center on the Eastern Shore of Maryland. From the various perspectives of their extensive experience, the invited participants discussed and debated a wide range of racial issues affecting higher education in general and the public colleges and universities in particular.

With the consent of the group, education writer John Egerton, who was present at the seminar, has drawn upon the conversations at Wye to prepare an essay on race and equity in higher education. The essay proceeds from a historical context to examine and interpret the diverse views of the conference participants. The American Council on Education now publishes this report and background papers in the conviction that the subject is vitally important to the nation's colleges and universities—and in the interest of drawing many more people into the continuing discussions.

J.W. Peltason

Preface

On February 16, 1973, U.S. District Judge John H. Pratt, in the case *Adams* v. *Richardson*, ordered the then Department of Health, Education and Welfare to demand of ten states compliance plans for the desegregation of their dual systems of higher education, as prohibited by Title VI of the Civil Rights Act of 1964, or to terminate federal funds to these states. In the nearly ten years since that order, of the ten states that submitted desegregation plans, none has achieved compliance. That stark recitation of fact represents both the failure and the promise of higher education desegregation.

The desegregative process in higher education is impeded by a complex of historical issues and social barriers that defy simple solution: decades of legally sanctioned, racially separate systems of public higher education; recalcitrant and obdurate state education authorities; long and arduous litigation and appeals; concerns of self-interest among both white and black educators; fears for the maintenance of identity of the historically black colleges in a context of desegregation; limited funds to truly "equalize" black and white universities; and even disagreement as to the definition of what constitutes a desegregated system of higher education. Nevertheless, despite the magnitude of the barriers, the process of desegregation goes forward. It has been ordered by the courts and it must be done. Whether it is done wisely or well, of course, depends on the wisdom, the skill, the tenacity and the goodwill of the key actors in the process. Bringing some of those key actors together to privately and candidly confront those complexities made considerable sense to a number of individuals in the summer of 1981.

In writing to the Ford Foundation requesting financial support for a seminar involving "higher education and desegregation leadership," J. W. Peltason, president of the American Council on

Education, noted that the meeting "would expect to produce specific suggestions which could be useful to the decision makers and might effect a change toward less contentious and more educationally productive directions. The proceedings would be off the record, but a document would be produced for circulation beyond the seminar.

"We would background the subject with four commissioned papers on the legal history of desegregation, on pertinent demographic and educational data, on the taxonomy of the segregated systems, and on different approaches to the enhancement of public black colleges. Our objectives would be to analyze the status of desegregation, the legal, educational and social issues and tensions surrounding the desegregation process and to search for wisdom and strategies to improve the process," Peltason added.

Acknowledgment for the successful implementation of the seminar must go initially to the leadership provided by President Peltason of the American Council and Francis Keppel of the Aspen Institute for Humanistic Studies. Key assistance in the planning was provided by James Jordan, Program Advisor at the American Council, Samuel Myers of the National Association for Equal Opportunity in Higher Education, David Tatel, formerly of the Department of Health, Education and Welfare and Leonard Haynes of the Office for the Advancement of Public Negro Colleges.

The Ford Foundation and its officers, Benjamin Payton and Gladys Chang Hardy, were generous in providing financial assistance for underwriting the seminar and supporting the publication of the proceedings. The Council's publication staff, Leonard Boswell and John Caldwell, provided invaluable production assistance under extremely stringent time constraints.

The present publication represents the product of the seminar. It is hoped that the seriousness, intensity, and determination of the participants and authors of papers is reflected in this manuscript, and that their reflection and dialogue will meaningfully impact on the ongoing litigation and negotiation of the process of desegregation.

The views of the authors, of course, are their own and do not represent the official positions of the agencies or institutions which employ them.

REGINALD WILSON

1 Race and Equity in Higher Education

John Egerton

In the winter of 1967, a group of education writers from around the country spent a week visiting public university campuses on a tour sponsored by the National Association of State Universities and Land-Grant Colleges. The writers pursued their own diverse interests on each campus, but all of them soon were struck by the high level of racial segregation they found, and somewhere along the way, they began to zero in on the issue. To one administrator and faculty member after another, the journalists posed such questions as these: Why is there so little racial integration in higher education? Why is segregation more pronounced in the biggest and best-known universities than in the smaller ones? What is this institution doing to aid in the nation's transition to an integrated society? If the best minds of this state are supposed to be here, and if those minds are trying to solve the toughest medical and agricultural and economic problems facing the nation, why aren't they also trying to solve the toughest social problems?

Feelings of frustration, shame, and anger were reflected in the answers to those questions: We're color-blind. We no longer make any distinctions based on race. Any qualified student or scholar is welcome here. Universities are not supposed to be instruments of social change. Integration would be too costly, or too far afield from our teaching and research missions, or too politically explosive. The responsibility properly belongs to other institutions, such as elementary and secondary schools. If we become centers of mass education, we can't maintain our quality or our prestige. Neither white nor black colleges and universities truly want to become fully integrated by race and socio-economic class.

Such exchanges were not uncommon then; the late 1960s were years of pervasive conflict in American higher education, and it was in that period that most colleges and universities came belatedly and often painfully to an acknowledgment of their own high degree of segregation. Not only in the South but in other parts of the country as well, there were clear indications that these institutions were less engaged in the desegregation process than were most elementary and secondary schools. In the largest traditionally white state universities from coast to coast, blacks accounted for fewer than two of every hundred students; in the historically black public colleges and universities, only about four of every hundred students were white.

Segregation—if not total exclusion of blacks and other minorities—has characterized most of the past decades and centuries of higher education in this country. In the first three hundred years of our post-Columbian history (during which Harvard was established as the first American college in 1636 and the University of Georgia was founded as the first state-supported institution of higher learning in 1785), educational opportunities at any level were virtually nonexistent for black people. For fully eighty years after the University of Georgia's creation, only a minuscule number of blacks gained entry to white colleges and universities, and only three small colleges for the black minority (Cheyney and Lincoln in Pennsylvania, Wilberforce in Ohio) managed to survive.

In the years following the Civil War, numerous public and private institutions for blacks were established, but the "separate but equal" doctrine promulgated by the United States Supreme Court in 1896 gave segregation the force of law and firmly established the patterns of exclusion and inequality that still existed, for all practical purposes, when the turbulent period of the late 1960s finally arrived.

A great many changes in the racial composition of colleges and universities have taken place since then. With due allowance for the ambiguity and imprecision of statistical summaries, the following very general figures provide a useful profile of the changing racial pattern:

	1960	*1970*	*1980*
Total Enrollment in Higher Education	4,000,000	8,000,000	12,000,000
Black Students in Higher Education	200,000	500,000	1,000,000

Blacks in Historically Black Institutions	130,000	170,000	200,000

Over the past two decades, the number of black students attending college has increased five-fold, and their proportion of the total higher education population has risen from 5 percent to more than 8 percent. In the same period, enrollment in the historically black colleges and universities has increased by more than 50 percent—yet only one of every five black students now attends a historically black institution, whereas two of every three did in 1960.

On the surface, these figures might be read as an indication that the larger issues of segregation and inequality have been settled, and that what remains are only a scattered few local and individual vestiges of discrimination. But on closer examination, it is apparent that the disputes and conflicts of the 1960s, while altered in tone and content, are still unresolved—and the debate continues.

At issue now is much more than the question of minority access to higher education. An increasingly complex and sophisticated set of problems and responses has evolved, and virtually all colleges and universities are now parties in the ongoing search for solutions. These are some of the circumstances that contribute to the issue of race in higher education in the 1980s:

- Traditionally white colleges and universities now enroll nearly four of every five black students—but traditionally black institutions still produce almost half of all black degree recipients.
- Despite large gains in recent years, blacks still make up only 8 percent of total college enrollment—though they are 14 percent of the college-age population.
- In all but a very few graduate and professional fields of study, the representation of black students and degree-holders has never risen above 2 percent.
- In spite of lawsuits and other challenges to segregation, some traditionally white universities have changed their racial complexion only slightly.
- A few historically black institutions, on the other hand, have become majority-white, and others are threatened by enrollment losses and funding cuts that some fear will be fatal unless they are soon halted.

- About half of all black college students are now enrolled in two-year institutions that collectively have a poor record of developing future recipients of undergraduate and advanced degrees.
- Attrition, a complex problem with many causes, affects a disproportionate percentage of black students at all levels of lower and higher education.
- A variety of factors, including rising costs, reductions in student financial aid, lawsuits against affirmative action programs, and a decline in the college-age population, may combine to produce a sharp drop in black enrollment on most campuses in the next few years.
- Not just enrollment but institutional survival of the black colleges is threatened by the prospects of diminished state and federal appropriations and private philanthropy in the current period of economic stagnation.
- In the makeup of most governing boards, administrations, and faculties and in the allocation of programs and funds, there remain many signs of continuing separation and inequality between white and black public institutions.

The list above is by no means an exhaustive compilation of contemporary racial concerns in American higher education, but it is representative enough to make the point that colleges and universities have not yet put the issues of discrimination and inequality to rest. And while the focus here is on black Americans—the largest and most visible of the nation's minority groups and the only one with a history of separate higher education institutions—the same trends and problems can be shown to pertain in varying degrees to other racial and ethnic minorities, and to the poor of all races.

Challenges to the "separate but equal" doctrine in education were first brought against colleges and universities almost fifty years ago—fully two decades before the U.S. Supreme Court, in its now-famous *Brown* decision of 1954, declared segregation laws to be unconstitutional. Between 1933 and 1938, black college students went to court in North Carolina, Virginia, Tennessee, Maryland, and Missouri seeking access to all-white graduate and professional schools. Only one of the petitioners, Donald Murray, was successful; he was admitted under a court order to the law school of the University of Maryland in 1936, and he subsequently graduated 12th in his class of 37 students.

In 1948 the Supreme Court decided an Oklahoma case, and in 1950 the court ruled in two cases from Texas; gradually and reluctantly, under judicial pressure, a few states began to lower the segregation barriers in their graduate and professional schools. Then came the *Brown* decision, and in the years that followed, lower federal courts ordered the admission of black undergraduate students to previously all-white state universities in Alabama, Georgia, Mississippi, and South Carolina.

By the time the Civil Rights Act of 1964 had been passed by Congress and signed into law by President Lyndon B. Johnson, thirty years of litigation and persistence had finally established the right of black students to enter previously all-white colleges and universities. But the right of access was only the first—and in retrospect the simplest—of the racial issues confronting American higher education.

In the fall of 1970, the NAACP Legal Defense and Educational Fund, Inc., a New York-based organization long engaged in civil rights litigation, filed a class action suit in the federal district court in Washington, charging that the U.S. Department of Health, Education, and Welfare had defaulted on its obligation to enforce Title VI of the Civil Rights Act of 1964. The plaintiffs were 31 students (suing through their parents) and two "citizens and taxpayers of the United States;" the defendants were Elliot L. Richardson, secretary of HEW, and other government officials. First on the alphabetical list of plaintiffs was John Quincy Adams of Brandon, Mississippi, suing on behalf of his six children. The case thus became known as *Adams* v. *Richardson*.

Title VI of the 1964 Civil Rights Act states that "No person in the United States shall, on the ground of race, color, or national origin, be excluded from participation in, or be denied the benefits of, or be subjected to discrimination under any program or activity receiving Federal financial assistance."

The lawsuit challenged HEW's continued financial assistance to a large number of public school systems and public higher education institutions known to be practicing segregation and discrimination. No state's federal funds have yet been cut off; even so, the portion of the *Adams* litigation pertaining to public higher education has had an enormous impact on scores of colleges and universities over the past decade. Although it has never reached the Supreme Court, *Adams* is a lawsuit of unprecedented controversy and consequence in American higher education.

The controversy has not only arisen between the interests of the states and those of the federal government; it has also been evident among civil rights groups and others concerned with the interests of minorities. Suffice it to say that in the voluminous exchanges of documents between the plaintiffs and the defendants over the past decade, the full range of issues concerning race in higher education has been examined in detail.

And yet, since February 1973, when Federal Judge John H. Pratt signed an order in favor of the *Adams* plaintiffs, the case has remained in active litigation and review. Ten of the nineteen states operating historically separate white and black institutions were subject to the original *Adams* ruling; the other nine have either been brought into the case since then or are parties in separate lawsuits. All of the states that once maintained dual systems of higher education thus are compelled now to develop and implement plans that will result in unitary systems serving blacks and whites equitably. They are further required to strengthen and enhance the historically black institutions, all of which have suffered from chronic discrimination and neglect. These requirements were spelled out by Judge Pratt, affirmed in June 1973 by the U.S. Court of Appeals for the District of Columbia, and finally agreed to by the defendants and the plaintiffs.

Nevertheless, *Adams* is still unsettled. Arguments continue over how well or how poorly the states are complying with the judicial imperative, over what the ruling requires of the white majority, and over what its ultimate consequences will be for black institutions, black faculty, and black students. Many who approve of *Adams* assert that it has not only expanded opportunities for blacks in traditionally white institutions but also improved the resources of traditionally black ones; others who are critical of the suit maintain that it has weakened some of the black institutions without increasing opportunities for black individuals elsewhere.

As one effort among many to reach a deeper understanding of the complexities involved in the issues of race and higher education, the American Council on Education and the Aspen Institute for Humanistic Studies convened a three-day seminar on the subject in mid-November of 1981. At the Wye Plantation conference center of the Aspen Institute on Maryland's Eastern Shore, the sponsors brought together a small group of university professors and administrators, state and federal government officials, attorneys, foundation executives, and others for an intensive exploration of racial issues, particularly as they pertain to the public sector of higher education. All of the approximately twenty-five people who attended have been directly engaged in one aspect or another of the desegregation process as it has evolved in courtrooms and on campuses during the past decade; some of them have had a continuing involvement in the issue for much longer than that.

The conversations were lively, provocative, and informative. No sweeping conclusions were drawn, but in the final hour of the seminar, the participants agreed to the issuance of a general report, in the interest of stimulating more discussions in larger academic, legal, and political circles. Their observations and comments are related below, without direct attribution.

Prior to the conference, the participants received six documents dealing with various aspects of the desegregation issue in higher education. Four of them were papers commissioned for the conference by ACE:

- "Toward the Desegregation and Effective Enhancement of Public Historically Black Institutions," by Albert H. Berrian, President of the Institute for Services to Education, Washington.
- "Demographics of Desegregation: The Status of Blacks in Higher Education," by James E. Blackwell, Professor of Sociology, University of Massachusetts, Boston.
- "A Perspective on the Constitutional Requirements for Desegregation of Higher Education," by Paul R. Dimond, Professor of Law, American University, Washington.
- "Toward a Political Taxonomy of Desegregating Higher Education," by Jewel L. Prestage, Professor of Political Science, Southern University, Baton Rouge.

The authors of these four papers made presentations at the conference and took part in the subsequent discussions.

The other two documents provided to the conferees were chapters from a forthcoming book on the predominantly black colleges and universities. The book, a joint project of ACE and the Council for the Advancement of Experiential Learning, is being edited by Morris T. Keeton and Stephen J. Wright. Taken from it for the benefit of the seminar were:

- An abstract and selected tables from "The Consequences of Federal and State Resources Allocations and Development Policies for Traditional Black Land-Grant Institutions, 1862–1954," a 1979 Ed.D. dissertation in the Harvard University Graduate School of Education by William E. Trueheart.
- "A Perspective on the Status and Prospects of the Public Black College," by Henry E. Cobb, Professor of History, Southern University, Baton Rouge.

The historical context provided by the Trueheart and Cobb papers laid the foundation for the conference presentations and the discussions that followed. Brief reviews of the four commissioned papers may now be useful here—as they were at the conference—to help bring the subsequent conversations and debates into sharp focus. The papers will be summarized in the following sequence: the current status of blacks in higher education (Blackwell, chapter 2), some consequences of the *Adams* litigation (Prestage, chapter 3), alternatives for further legal action (Dimond, chapter 4), and the future of the black colleges and universities (Berian, chapter 5).

James E. Blackwell, in his study of black participation in higher education, cited an abundance of statistical data to show that over the past four decades, blacks have made impressive advances in educational achievement. In 1940, only one of every ten blacks age 25 to 34 had completed high school; by 1975, seven of every ten had done so. Between 1950 and 1975, the percentage of blacks age 18 to 24 who were enrolled in college more than quadrupled, and in the same period, there was an increase of nearly 350 percent in the number of blacks who had completed four or more years of college. "It is still extremely difficult for blacks to close the educational gap between themselves and whites in the United States," Mr. Blackwell wrote. "But the gap is closing."

Nevertheless, he continued, blacks are still disproportionately under-represented in most compilations of higher educational achievement. An alarmingly high black dropout rate is indicated in secondary schools as well as colleges: in 1977, nearly one-fourth of all 18- to 24-year-old blacks were classified as high school dropouts, and in 1979 it was reported that only 17 of every 100 black freshmen go on to complete four years of college. The white attrition rate is roughly half that of blacks.

A major portion of the increase in black higher education enrollment in recent years has been recorded in two-year institutions; fully half of all black students attend such schools. Citing Florida as a prime example of this trend, Mr. Blackwell noted that between 1970 and 1976, there was an increase of nearly 10 percent (to better than six of every ten) in the proportion of black college students in that state who were enrolled in junior colleges, and the proportion has continued to climb since then. Only about one-third of all black graduates of community colleges in Florida make a successful transition to four-year institutions.

In round numbers, there were about a million blacks enrolled in college in 1980: 60 percent in traditionally white institutions, 20 percent in traditionally black ones, and the remaining 20 percent in colleges and universities identified as "newer predominantly black institutions"—urban public colleges and universities of recent origin, for the most part. The enrollment shift to this new category of colleges and to the majority-white schools, Mr. Blackwell wrote, has cut deeply into enrollment at the historically black institutions, and underscores their need for increased public support as a means of assuring the maintenance and enrichment of their contributions and their quality.

These additional contemporary trends and developments were noted in the Blackwell paper:

- A recent decline in the number and proportion (to roughly 60,000 and 6 percent) of black students enrolled in graduate and professional schools;
- An increase of black students in business, engineering, and the sciences—but a continuing under-representation of blacks (barely 2 percent) among recent graduates in those fields;
- A doubling of the number of doctoral degrees awarded to blacks between 1973 and 1979 (from 581 to 1,055)—yet blacks still receive no more than five of every 100 doctorates, and three out of four of them are in the overcrowded fields of education and the social sciences;
- A tiny representation of blacks on the faculties of traditionally white institutions (among all the faculties of such schools in eight of the *Adams* states surveyed in 1977, a mere 1.6 percent were black);

- A continuing low proportion of black graduates from most of the professional schools of formerly all-white universities. (The few existing professional schools in black institutions not only produce the lion's share of black professionals but a generous number of white graduates as well. One example: in 1976, the school of veterinary medicine at traditionally white Auburn University in Alabama had no blacks at all in its graduating class—but the 40 veterinarians produced that year by traditionally black Tuskegee Institute in the same state included 14 whites.)

In his conclusion, Mr. Blackwell called for a concerted effort to increase the enrollment, graduation, and employment of blacks in all levels of higher education, to the end that black students, graduates, and employees will be equitably represented in all colleges and universities, in the professional ranks, and in the skilled labor force.

Jewel L. Prestage noted in her study of higher education desegregation that black land-grant colleges in the late nineteenth century were the earliest institutional expressions of the white majority's determination to compel racial segregation. Elevation of the myth of "separate but equal" to the status of a constitutional principle was accomplished by the U.S. Supreme Court in the *Plessy* v. *Ferguson* decision of 1896—and by that time, 27 separate and unequal institutions for blacks had been established in 17 states.

The "equal protection" clause of the Fourteenth Amendment was the primary basis for legal challenges to segregation in higher education in the years prior to the *Brown* case, and it remained so until Title VI of the Civil Rights Act of 1964 prohibited all forms of racial segregation in institutions receiving federal funds. Now it is Title VI (as well as the Constitution) that provides the legal framework for the *Adams* litigation—and it was the desegregation plans of six of the *Adams* states (Louisiana, South Carolina, North Carolina, Arkansas, Georgia, Florida) that provided the major focus for Ms. Prestage's Baper.

Specifically, she examined the government's criteria for developing desegregation plans and the responses of the states to five of the criteria: disestablishment of the dual system of institutions; desegregation of student enrollment; desegregation of faculty, administrative staffs, non-academic personnel, and governing boards; enhancement of historically black institutions; and monitoring and reporting on plan implementation. At the conclusion of her review, Ms. Prestage made these observations:

- Program enhancement proposals for the black colleges frequently call for the addition of undergraduate and graduate programs in education—the chosen field of a majority of blacks who hold advanced degrees, but also the field of least current demand. Some new programs in which blacks are under-represented should be assigned to black institutions—but these should be in traditional disciplines rather than in unproven experimental programs.
- Wherever white and black public institutions exist in close proximity to each other, their duplicate programs make it difficult if not impossible to achieve satisfactory levels of biracial participation. Such duplication should be directly addressed in the state plans.
- An acceptable balance of blacks and whites on the faculties of all public institutions cannot be achieved without faculty salary equalization. This subject needs more attention in most of the states.
- Specific numerical goals for student enrollment in all affected institutions should be made an integral part of each plan, and scholarship and support services to help attain those goals should be based on demonstrated need and not on an artificial numerical parity.
- Faculty development at predominantly black institutions should go beyond support for completion of terminal degrees to include support for postdoctoral study and research, program and course development, and sabbatical leaves.
- All plans developed by the states should provide for the highest level of participation by outside institutions and groups of citizens in the assessment and reporting of progress in implementation.

Finally, Ms. Prestage noted that the best of plans is of only limited value unless it is integrated into the state planning progress and assured of budgetary support. Proper planning, adequate funding, and the personal commitment of educational and political leaders are in the final analysis indispensible elements in the achievement of racial equity in higher education.

Paul R. Dimond's paper for the Wye conference was a treatise on legal and constitutional principles in response to segregation and discrimination in higher education. Despite decades of litigation, he wrote, very little case law and no specific constitutional principles have been developed on "the wrong of official racial discrimination" in higher education and a commensurate remedy for it. Mr. Dimond set about to examine two such principles and the remedies suggested by them. The two principles, or constitutional rules, as he stated them are:

- "A state that has in the past restricted access to higher education on a racial basis . . . bears the affirmative duty to insure that black applicants who can benefit from higher education are no longer effectively excluded."
- "A state that has in the past imposed mandatory segregation in its system of higher education bears the affirmative duty to implement a plan of actual desegregation that, subject to the practicalities of the local situation, (a) will work to convert to a unitary system . . . (b) realistically begins . . . to overcome any residual effects of the former dual schooling, and (c) does not pick disproportionately on identifiably black as compared to white interests to bear the brunt of any remedial burdens."

The first of these, said Mr. Dimond, is a principle of individual remedy; its aim is to guarantee access to higher education for individual blacks who aspire to it and possess the necessary qualifications or potential. The second is a principle of group relief from class segregation. Both rules assume a constitutional violation that requires affirmative relief rather than racial neutrality that would perpetuate the violation. The fundamental constitutional question that must be resolved now, the author wrote, is whether only the access rule or the principle of group relief as well should now apply to public systems of higher education.

Reviewing the history of elementary and secondary school segregation cases, Mr. Dimond concluded that "group discrimination against blacks as a class (as well as denial to individuals of meaningful access to particular schools) is prohibited by the Constitution." But the tension between theories of group relief and individual access has not been resolved for higher education; the Supreme Court has not spoken on the subject, and no lower court decisions have given a clear sense of direction. Absent such guidance, Mr. Dimond made these observations:

- The access principle promises no relief (beyond recruiting of talented students) for increasing the number of blacks at historically white institutions, and there is even some doubt now—because of the Supreme Court's opinions in "reverse discrimination" cases—about the manner and extent to which any state may seek voluntarily to increase the diversity of its traditionally white schools by admitting blacks whose credentials are deemed to be less competitive than those of some whites.
- The access principle also does not require states that formerly mandated segregation to upgrade the facilities, faculties, curriculum, or mission of their historically black institutions; it requires only that white and black schools henceforth be funded according to a race-neutral principle that makes no allowance for past discrimination.
- The access principle, because it depends on the political process rather than a constitutional standard to resolve differences, is very attractive to states that want the least disruption of higher education, to blacks who want to save black schools, and to courts looking for a principled way out of a potentially divisive issue.
- The lower federal courts and the individual members of the Supreme Court are far from consensus on the conflicting principles of group relief and individual access.

Mr. Dimond made clear his own support for the group relief principle in his concluding remarks, saying that his "litigation instinct" suggests that "the current racial identification of most colleges and universities can be traced in substantial part and significant detail to the continuing effects of dual schooling pre-*Brown* and to the perpetuation of the basic racial division post-*Brown*." Further, "the voluntary nature of student application and matriculation and faculty decisions in higher education does not necessarily limit constitutional analyses to the individual access rather than the group discrimination principle." The various parties interested in eliminating all vestiges of segregation and discrimination in higher education, said Mr. Dimond, "should be actively considering the merits and potential of much more wide-ranging and novel class relief."

Albert H. Berrian, in his conference paper, examined the current state of historically black public institutions and suggested ways to strengthen them. He noted that the *Adams* litigation and other desegregation initiatives have highlighted a "capability gap" in those institutions, and they continue to lose ground in the present period of retrenchment and austerity. Only Howard University among all public and private historically black institutions has a comprehensive research and development capability; none of the schools is a major provider of services and expertise to third world nations; few are equipped to provide public or extension services at home; only three—all private—are training allied health professionals and delivering health care services.

The small number of graduate and professional-school programs in black institutions and the historic exclusion of blacks from programs in traditionally white institutions have resulted in a dearth of black architects, engineers, economists, mathematicians, physicists, chemists—barely more than 1 percent of the national totals—and the numbers are almost as low for medicine and law, in spite of the fact that most black doctors and lawyers in the country are graduates of the three medical schools and three law schools in black institutions.

Mr. Berrian's objective was not to dwell upon existing inequities but to suggest ways to equalize institutional and individual opportunities, and his principal suggestion was for "a monitored, integrated approach to developmental education." Cooperative planning by local, state, and federal entities is vital to the development of programs in which under-prepared students are systematically trained to acquire the verbal, quantitative, and scientific skills required of all graduate and professional-school students. Effective programs of this kind, Mr. Berrian wrote, may now be more prevalent in traditionally white institutions than in historically black ones: "It is not true that historically black institutions are better equipped to provide developmental services or that they are more prone to do so. Efforts in this regard have been carefully examined . . . and no indication has been found that historically white institutions, once committed to the developmental education concept, are less adept at mounting successful programs than black institutions."

Since only 20 percent of all black students are now in traditionally black institutions, and since numerically more whites than blacks are in need of developmental education, it is both necessary and proper for predominantly white institutions to have this capability. Nevertheless, such programs are still vital in the historically black institutions, said Mr. Berrian, and the future development of those institutions may depend in large measure on their capacity to deliver instruction and counseling that will help under-prepared students to close the gaps in their learning and prepare themselves for advanced study.

Neither the federal government, the states, nor the higher education community has an enviable record of support for racial equity in colleges and universities, or for large-scale programs of developmental education; the racial and socio-economic divisions have been left more or less in place until recently. Mr. Berrian, in calling for cooperation and change, said in his paper that the various interested parties must work together to overcome past and present inequities. Developmental education, he said, will pose difficult and persistent problems, and it will be expensive; it is, nevertheless, unavoidable if students with special needs are to be treated justly and humanely.

As one possible step toward change, Mr. Berrian recommended creation of a human resources development center at one of the traditionally black institutions. Such a center would have an interdisciplinary staff engaged in applied research on the problems of developing under-served and under-productive human populations.

In nearly 24 hours of formal and informal discussion, the participants in the Wye conference went beyond the background papers to consider a broad range of general and specific issues of race in higher education. The conversation began with an examination of Paul Dimond's two constitutional principles governing remedy for segregation: individual access and group relief.

An accepted philosophy or way of viewing the constitutional requirements for ending segregation and discrimination in higher education has not yet been developed, even though desegregation cases in universities were first initiated a half-century ago. Those early cases sought individual access remedies; the *Brown* case first established the principle of class or group remedy in elementary and secondary schools, and *Adams* has since sought to do likewise in higher education. But *Adams* has not reached the Supreme Court, and there are at present no cases in the lower courts that appear likely to lead to the establishment of a firm constitutional philosophy for defining the wrong and determining relief.

In the Dimond scenario, the first principle—individual access—would simply require non-discrimination in admissions; higher education would be treated as a unique institution (neither free nor compulsory, as elementary and secondary schools are), and the courts would guarantee only the right of individuals to equal consideration for entry. There would be no compulsion for states to rectify past inequities, and in such a circumstance, the historically black institutions might in time wither on the vine and be closed.

The second principle—the group or class violation and remedy—would require statewide solutions to segregation and inequality; historically black institutions would have to be upgraded to parity with white schools, and a unitary system unidentifiable by race would evolve. The racial heritage of individual institutions might well survive and be highly valued, but no school would be inferior to others in any racial sense.

A flurry of questions was then raised: Is the individual access remedy a smokescreen behind which historically black institutions will be eliminated? Could the group remedy be used to disestablish newer predominantly white colleges that have been planted near traditionally black ones? Is it best to actively pursue a constitutional remedy or to leave the issue alone and let it resolve itself in the political process? Isn't the government actually compelling the *Adams* states to move toward group relief? Isn't the Supreme Court now deeply divided over this very philosophical choice, and isn't it leaning toward the more conservative individual access theory?

The history of the judicial process, said one speaker, suggests that if *Adams* is allowed to run its course, the present muddled situation will eventually give way to a clear solution to both the individual and group rights questions. There is some value in the process, and for all the risks and problems involved, we would be well advised to stay on the legal course, to take the initiative whenever possible, and to be patient.

But, came the reply, *Adams* is not the vehicle for reaching a settlement of these issues, because a "victory" in *Adams* simply means that the Department of Education is required to negotiate a remedy with the offending state. Neither *Adams* nor any other case on the horizon will settle the constitutional questions at issue anytime soon, it was argued—and in the absence of a judicial settlement, only political solutions will be possible.

In the exchange of opinions that followed, two schools of thought emerged. The first can be summarized in this way: it's a little late to be talking now about legal strategies when the race issue in higher education is moving away from the courts and toward political and educational resolution. Furthermore, even the speculation that some of the public black colleges might be closed is a negative and defeatist thought that could become a self-fulfilling prophecy. We ought to be talking about developing all existing institutions for the good of the whole society, and especially about upgrading the historically black institutions to parity. There have been too many lawyers in this fight for too long; it's time now for institutional leaders to work out cooperative solutions, and time for the political process to produce some constructive compromises.

The second collective viewpoint included these thoughts: A solution by policy and political action may leave the traditionally black institutions more vulnerable than they are now, and with no latitude and no recourse. The political route might be faster, and it could even produce fair solutions in some states, but it would be very uneven and unpredictable, and it might result in the loss of some black institutions and a net loss of black students. Most states would accept the individual access solution, but it would open the historically black institutions to "non-racial" decisions that favor the white majority and the upper socioeconomic classes—standardized tests, cuts in student financial aid, formula funding based on enrollment, meritocracy in all its forms. The best strategy now is to work hard for the group-relief philosophy in the courts. In the *Adams* states and in any other cases that can be moved forward, we need to be constructing a group-relief model of equity among institutions and greater access and success for minorities in all institutions. The group remedy automatically incorporates the individual's right of access; the group-relief principle in higher education needs to be embedded in constitutional law, and that is the strategy that educators and lawyers and politicians who believe in equality should be pursuing.

The discussion underscored the peril of both political and judicial strategies for securing equity in higher education; neither negotiation nor litigation can guarantee a favorable result. In fact, as varied as were the interpretations of the problem and its possible solutions, there was an implied consensus that black institutions and individuals are losing momentum in the struggle for equality, no matter which strategy they pursue.

That conclusion is supported by demographic shifts in enrollment over the past five years: a rapidly rising proportion of black students in two-year colleges, a general decline in enrollment at both public and private historically black institutions, and a drop in the number of black students in graduate and professional schools.

The inability or unwillingness of graduate and professional schools in most fields to accommodate an equitable percentage of blacks or other minorities was a subject of extended discussion in the Wye seminar. Blacks are proportionally nearly three times as numerous in the nation's population as they are in each year's output of new doctorates and professional degree recipients. In specific disciplines, these current conditions were noted:

- There has been a five-fold increase in the annual number of new black physicians over the past decade, but in that same period only 4.2 percent of the 140,000 medical school graduates were black. Now there is a leveling off, and in some cases a decline, in the number of black first-year medical students, indicating that a smaller number and percentage will be represented in future classes. In addition, the cost of medical education and the lessening of student financial aid and other forms of federal assistance pose serious problems for black medical students in general and for the three predominantly black medical schools in particular. If the traditionally white medical schools served blacks as well as the schools at Howard, Meharry, and Morehouse serve whites, the past decade's output of black physicians would have been three or four times greater than it was.
- More than half of the black enrollees and graduates in the nation's schools of pharmacy each year are associated with four predominantly black institutions—and again, white participation in those schools far exceeds black involvement in the predominantly white institutions.
- In social work, the only discipline in which parity of black involvement has been achieved in the past, there is now an indication that the percentage of black enrollees and graduates has peaked and fallen.
- In law as in medicine, the increase in black enrollment at traditionally white institutions came during a period of gen-

eral enrollment expansion and left the percentage of blacks in the profession relatively unchanged. Now, amid talk of a surplus of lawyers (and doctors), enrollments are stabilizing or declining, and the decline is more apparent among blacks than whites. There may be too many doctors and lawyers as a whole, observed one conferee, but there still are not enough black doctors and lawyers.

- In the arts and sciences, the low numbers of black doctorates characterize almost every discipline, and the resulting Ph.D. output is too small to supply universities and government agencies and industries with the numbers they need to achieve meaningful integration. Furthermore, the relatively few black Ph.D.s produced by predominantly white institutions tend to come disproportionately from a small number of departments which have earned a reputation for including black faculty and students in their programs. In some fields—political science, for example—over half of all graduate departments never have awarded the Ph.D. to a black student.

In summary, the graduate and professional schools remain overwhelmingly white; the modest trend toward diversity that began in the late 1960s has now passed its apex, and very few traditionally white graduate departments or professional schools have more than a small fraction of black students, faculty members, or graduates. Traditionally black institutions still produce more than their share of baccalaureate- and advanced-degree recipients who are black.

The racial changes that have taken place in higher education in the past dozen years or so have been greater than in all the earlier decades combined. Yet two ironic conclusions emerge: The first is that in a time of growth, blacks gained numerically but seldom relatively; they remain underrepresented in colleges and universities—and now, in a time of retrenchment, they face an even greater loss of equity. The second is that while the end of legalized segregation did bring about some change in the racial composition of most colleges and universities, it has not arrested the large and growing advantage that white institutions generally have held over black ones.

Circumstances differ from state to state, from institution to institution, and even from department to department. Some state systems of higher education have made genuine progress in converting their once-segregated campuses into a single network benefitting all; others seem determined to maintain a high degree of separation; still others apparently intend to eliminate the historically black institutions. Legal strategies have been dominant in some states, political strategies in others—and in a sense, a combination of the two has tended to prevail in all. In and out of the *Adams* litigation, states have tended to reshape their higher education systems according to the dictates of history, politics, state and federal law, personalities, geography, demographics—and last and least, educational philosophy. There is no explaining the widely divergent outcomes in states of ostensibly similar circumstance, except to say that the blend of actors and scripts contained subtle variations—and produced different dramas.

Louisiana is a case in point. It was one of the original states in the *Adams* suit, but Louisiana officials refused to submit a desegregation plan to the federal government, contending that the state no longer operated a dual system of higher education. The U.S. Department of Justice sued the state separately. After six years of maneuvering highlighted by a confusing succession of proposals and counterproposals from all parties in the dispute, a legal and political settlement was finally negotiated by federal and state officials in 1981.

As different as all the states responses to *Adams* have been, Louisiana's may have been the most different of all. Its governor, David Treen, played a prominent and decisive role in the final negotiations with federal representatives; the result, in the words of one observer, was "a legal-political compromise, a series of power swaps and tradeoffs" that left some institutions unaffected, some salary differentials in place, and all existing academic programs untouched.

Yet for all its differences, the Louisiana compromise was reminiscent in some ways of others: It involved weary negotiators, overwhelmed by the sheer volume of paperwork, seeing no clear consensus among blacks or whites, settling in the end for plans that prolong the status quo and consent decrees that produce little real change.

What difference, then, has *Adams* made? What if there had been no *Adams* lawsuit? Among the conferees, responses to those questions varied widely. Some said nothing at all has changed as a direct result of the litigation; others contended that black institutions and black students are in a more threatened position now than before, and still others asserted that some black institutions would already be closed and many fewer black students would have entered and completed higher education had it not been for the legal challenge to dual systems in the states. The questions can never be answered with certainty, of course, but this much is clear: The participation of blacks in higher education has increased substantially since 1970, and the *Adams* suit is a major reason for the increase. The effect of *Adams* on the black colleges is less clear—but there, too, it seems likely that the status of some of them might have diminished had it not been for the court decision requiring their enhancement.

The plight of the public black institutions in the past and at present was a topic of special concern and sensitivity to the Wye conferees, who found it difficult to speak of the schools' strengths without sounding too laudatory—or of their weaknesses without sounding too critical. In the discussion of Albert Berrian's paper and at other points during the seminar, it was apparent that the future of the public black institutions was a matter of overriding importance.

It is the practice of many who are familiar with the public black colleges to speak primarily of their traditions, their strengths, and their assets, the better to defend them from critics and to advocate their preservation and perpetuation. There are thirty-five public black colleges and universities in nineteen states, and the differences among them tend to be overshadowed by their common history as schools for blacks; defenders and critics alike, albeit for different reasons, often speak of the thirty-five institutions as if they were identical and inseparable.

In this collective view that accentuates traditions and strengths, the public black colleges are seen as schools that have struggled against overwhelming odds to educate tens of thousands of the nation's most successful black people. Perpetually underfunded and shunted aside in the era of segregation, they had to make do with far less than the all-white schools—and they have more than made do: For over a century, they and their sister institutions in the private sector have not only produced the lion's share of the nation's black college graduates but most of the black doctors, lawyers, and academicians as well. Even now, the public black colleges and universities graduate nearly one-fourth of all the black students who earn degrees each year.

That such a record requires defense is seen by many knowledgeable students of race and education as an indication of white society's failure to recognize and appreciate the contributions of these institutions. They assert that the black colleges are a rich national resource, a past and present asset to black citizens and to the nation in general, and an asset of great future importance as well.

There are others, equally as proud of this record, who tend to emphasize the needs and weaknesses of the public black institutions in order to insist that they be raised to parity with the historically white institutions in their states. Here, in summary, is an interpretation of that point of view:

The public black institutions historically have been victimized by segregation and discrimination and inequality. It is a sham to speak only of their strengths and to say they are equal; they are not. None of them has ever had a medical school or a broad Ph.D. program; none has become a real university in the fullest sense. They have no great research strengths, few public service programs, little impact in the larger community or in third-world nations abroad. White institutions are producing almost all of the nation's future engineers, scientists, and technologists. There are sixteen public black land-grant institutions, yet not one of them has graduate programs in agriculture that are relevant to the modern age. Even in such traditional fields as education and nursing, the black institutions are not producing the specialists who can be influential in shaping tomorrow's schools and health-care institutions. It is a travesty of justice to allow these inequities to continue. In the interest of simple fairness—and for the benefit of black and white Americans in the future—these institutions should be given the resources to develop to their fullest potential. There are individuals and even programs in all of the public black colleges that are excellent by any measure, but they are outstanding in spite of their circumstances, not because of them. In any serious program of institutional development, it is inevitable that these indigenous strengths will attract support faster and make the most of it when it comes; thus, some of the colleges may rise faster than others, and it may turn out that some will become genuine universities while others languish. But those consequences are unpredictable. For the moment, what is required is opportunity, and resources; then, it will be up to each institution to demonstrate the quality and productivity that future survival will demand.

The suggestion that some public black institutions are stronger than others, or that some may flourish while others fade, is a controversial notion not often discussed in higher education circles. Even in the Wye conference, most speakers addressed the issue obliquely—but it was discussed, and the questions and comments below are a sample of what was said:

"Who should decide which institutions get the most support and the best chance to become competitive? Who will take the political risk?"

"Whoever has the financial and political power and the nerve to act."

"No institution can expand in these difficult economic times. The way to proceed is not to single out a few institutions for special development, but for each state to do the best we can with the ones we're responsible for."

"We've had opportunities and let them pass, built new white institutions while old black ones withered on the vine. Now, one way or the other, we're going to pay dearly for the inequities we've created."

"Does the past performance of any of the public black colleges merit the confidence required to build a few great institutions?"

"They've done well with what they've had; the problem is, they haven't had enough. Now, with or without *Adams*, regardless of what we do or don't do, a few of the institutions—maybe seven or eight—are going to rise to the top of the heap and have a chance to become real universities in a class with the flagship institutions. They *could* do it, that is, if the resources were made available."

"But where will the resources come from? The federal commitment for such an undertaking simply isn't there, and never has been—and who could name a state with the wealth and the commitment to do it?"

"The states have always managed to find the resources to build strength on strength at the white institutions, but no serious effort has been made anywhere to assure a black college of truly equal and competitive status. It's not a matter of wealth. Underneath, I think it's still a matter of race."

"Even in their own projections, not a single one of the public black institutions anticipates or even dreams of being a large multiversity with, say, 20,000 students and a full range of graduate programs. Their self-perception is limited. Some would say that's realism; others would call it a lack of vision."

"We may see a few of the colleges surge forward and become major institutions, but that will depend more on internal initiatives than on external forces. Creative leadership and political sophistication will determine the big gainers. It was dynamic leaders and entrepreneurs that lifted many of the white schools to prominence after World War II, and the emergence of such people in the public black colleges will be a primary factor in their growth."

"It would take a redistribution of state and national resources in education to accomplish a restructuring of the public black institution. It would be a risky game, a purely political contest. But the hard truth is that the lot of every one of these institutions is now vitally dependent upon the political process. We have a hard choice between trying to save all of them, or concentrating resources to develop a few truly competitive universities. The courts aren't going to make this choice. It's up to politicians and lawyers and educators in the states to make it."

"Is the real issue the survival of the public black colleges, or is it the evolution of a higher education system that compensates for past inequities and provides the fullest and fairest opportunities for all in a diverse family of institutions indivisible by race?"

"It's really very simple: The public black colleges do exist; they should; they must. There is no way to justify the closing of a single one of them, and I wouldn't want my name associated with anyone who still questions their right to exist. They simply must exist—and serve all."

"But serving all will ultimately mean white majorities in most of these schools. Even in Mississippi, which has a highest black population in the nation, nearly two-thirds of the people are white. If the formerly white institutions are brought by force or by choice to an acceptable level of integration, the black institutions will have to do the same, and in time there will be no more public black institutions."

"No, there will still be institutions, and they will be stronger and more competitive than they are now; they just wouldn't be majority black."

"The key issue is expanding opportunity for black students;

there is a responsibility in that for the traditionally white institutions, and a role for the traditionally black ones."

"The principal issue is full support for black colleges."

"No, the principal issue is guaranteeing education of the highest quality for all."

"A majority of the black students are already in predominantly white institutions. Instead of putting so much emphasis on the future of the public black colleges, we need to make sure the white ones don't get off the hook. We have to hold their feet to the fire, and make them open up; they won't do it without pressure."

"The bottom line is productivity. If we expand opportunities for blacks in all the institutions, we can double or triple the production of graduates in various fields at every level. That's the goal—or should be: not desegregation, but production. When I see real growth, I'll be less concerned about who goes where. We ought to give every institution an opportunity to produce—and then let the unproductive ones, white or black, fall by the wayside."

The conversation was spirited and penetrating. It carried over from the formal session to the dinner tables and on into the evening. If there was no clear set of answers expressed and no consensus found, there was at least a start made toward framing the right questions and opening them up to critical examination.

In the final morning of the seminar, an effort was made to draft a document of "assumptions for the next decade"—in effect, a statement of principal issues and priorities. The effort stimulated further sharp debate and discussion, but in the end, no statement was written to represent the views of the group. In truth, none could have been, for the views were too diverse. Again, some excerpted comments may capture the tone and flavor of the conversation:

"Any statement speculating on the possible closing of some institutions will be interpreted by some as an endorsement of such a move. At best, many people see the only role for black institutions as doing for black students those things that white institutions cannot or will not do: mainly, trying to help the minorities, the poor, the marginal students. I'd like to see the black institutions given credit for what they've done *without* resources—and an expression of confidence that they can be first rate with enhancement. They have done so much for so many with so little."

"The states are still operating dual systems of higher education. Segregation still exists. We need to spell out roles and responsibilities for all parties in the continuing desegregation process."

"We ought to quit saying segregation still exists. It was forced separation required by law, and that's over. Racism still exists, but desegregation has been accomplished."

"No—desegregation is a process, and it is ongoing."

"The historically black institutions have to be given responsibility for operating high-level, high-quality programs that will attract top students, black and white. To the extent of their ability, they should share in the kinds of programs that now exist only in the flagship universities."

"White institutions won't give up such programs. No institution will surrender programs without a fight."

"The states aren't going to start expensive new programs, either—not now, anyway. We want desperately to get the most black faculty and students we can into our medical school, but we can't afford to build a new one."

"But there's a new medical school in Louisiana, and one in Tennessee. White institutions expand—it's only black ones that don't. You say we have to be practical, reasonable; I say we have to be bold. The reasonable folks won't end up with much."

"You just keep talking numbers, quantitative measures. But what about quality? The white institutions have a serious problem in trying to attract blacks to their faculties or to their graduate and professional schools. The best ones have plenty of offers, and the worst ones simply aren't prepared. The pool of candidates isn't large enough—and that's the fault of all undergraduate schools, white and black. As for the black institutions, rightly or wrongly, there's a public perception that their programs are of lower quality and their degrees less meaningful."

"If the definition of quality was based on exit standards, not entry standards, the black colleges would have a much better reputation. The relative quality of their programs has suffered because of the history of racism, but based on the value-added concept—student improvement between admission and graduation—they've done a very good job."

"Still, we've got to get over the notion that all historically black public institutions must survive as black institutions. They're there to serve an end, and that end is not self-perpetuation—it's the education of students, whatever their race."

"Regardless of how you feel about institutions, these arguments may all be academic if the student financial aid problem continues to get worse. Without financial aid, 90 percent of the black students now in college would be forced out, and the same is true of Hispanics, native Americans, and poor whites. The United States has never had sharp class divisions in its educational structure, as England and most European countries have—but the fear now is that we are headed that way. Private financial aid and many state programs as well are based on patterns of discrimination that favor whites. Federal programs have not been like that—now those programs are being curtailed sharply, and there is even a new attitude in government that seems to say if you take $100 each from a rich man and a poor man, you've treated them equally. If that attitude prevails, neither black institutions nor black individuals will have a chance to overcome the effects of past discrimination."

In the end, the American Council on Education/Aspen Institute seminar on desegregation in higher education closed without settling any of the perplexing issues before it. It had no authority to resolve the issues, of course—and in any event, settlement was not the objective. But the discussions did permit a candid and thorough exploration of the issues, and in the exchange of views there was considerable value. The institutional and individual objectives of equity for blacks and other minorities in higher education were debated at length; the roles and responsibilities of federal, state, and local governments, of courts and politicians and educators, were examined from various points of view. A greater appreciation for the complexity of the issues—and for the divergent opinions expressed—may have resulted. If there is no agreement now, no consensus, perhaps there is at least some clarification of what is in dispute and what is at stake. And in these pages recounting the discussions, perhaps there are also some insights and some facts that will be of value to others in higher education who seek now to make colleges and universities more equitable and more productive for all segments of American society.

2 Demographics of Desegregation

James E. Blackwell

Eight decades into the twentieth century and more than a dozen decades following the end of legalized slavery in the United States, the nation has not achieved equality of educational opportunity for all its citizens. Although there is significant evidence that progress has been made toward the realization of equal opportunity in education, much more has to be accomplished before educational parity is attained.

The primary purpose of this paper is to present descriptive data that show the current status of black Americans in higher education. Although special attention is more often given to black-white comparisons, the underrepresentation of other minorities in American higher education today is also recognized. It is only because of limitations of space that more attention is not devoted to an assessment of the conditions of other minority groups in higher education. In this discussion, however, the primary foci are (1) selected demographic factors pertinent to the understanding of the current status of blacks in the desegregation process; (2) desegregation in community colleges, four-year colleges and universities and in graduate/professional schools; (3) desegregation in the Adams-Califano/Bell States; (4) desegregation and the crucial role of the historically black colleges; and (5) black faculty and administrators.

The author has relied on a number of highly illuminating data sources, some of which are pieces of original research while others are essentially secondary sources. Heavy reliance is made here on data from the U.S. Census Bureau, the National Center for Education Statistics, reports published by the National Advisory Committee on Black Higher Education and Black Colleges and Universities, studies published by the Southern Education Foundation and the Southern Regional Education Board, and others.

Age, Sex, Income, and Schooling Among Black Americans

Correlates of high educational attainment include such variables as age, sex, income, and race. For instance, until quite recently, more men than women were enrolled in colleges and universities. Because of high educational costs, the economically advantaged were more likely to complete all levels of education than were the economically disadvantaged. The number and proportions of white Americans who completed high school, attended and completed college, and received graduate/professional degrees far surpassed such graduates among the black population. Race and sex distinctions in schooling rates are changing, though not at the same speed. In some areas, however, there is disturbing evidence of retrogression following a sustained period in which gaps in education attributed to differences in race and income had begun to close.

It is traditional to regard the "college-going" age cohorts as those persons who fall between the ages of eighteen and twenty-two. In some instances, to make allowances for high achievers, the range is set at ages 16–22 years. However, because of the declining numbers of eighteen-year-olds in the population and the return of older men and women to college, and persons who comprise the nontraditional college-going group (e.g., older persons whose college education was interrupted by other careers, motherhood, or war), the college-going population has been expanded to include persons of ages 18–34. All three ranges are cited in various studies of the demographic characteristics of students in higher education systems. In fact, as this paper unfolds, it is likely that reference will be made not only to three already identified age cohorts but to others as well.

According to U.S. Census Bureau data, blacks have made impressive advances in the number of years of schooling achieved. When the Bureau first began collecting data on race and schooling in 1940, only one of every ten blacks aged 25–34 was a high school graduate. In 1969, the proportion in the same age cohort was approximately three of every ten. However, by 1975, the proportion for black persons in this age group who had completed high school reached seven of every ten (U.S. Census Bureau, 1978, 87). In the thirty-five year period between 1940 and 1975, the educational differences between blacks and whites were narrowed primarily as a result of the more rapid increase in the proportion of blacks who completed high school in com-

...at for white persons during the same period (U.S. ...u, 1978, 87).

...arly, despite the persistence of high dropout rates among blacks, their college-going rates have also substantially increased during the past decades. Census data show that the "proportion of black men and women 18–24 years old enrolled in colleges increased only slightly in the 1950s and then rose sharply in the 1960–70 decade." (Table 1).

TABLE 1

PERSONS 18 TO 24 YEARS OLD ENROLLED IN COLLEGE BY RACE AND SEX, FOR SELECTED YEARS BETWEEN 1950 and 1975 (Numbers in Thousands)

Enrollment Status, Sex and Race	1950*	1960*	1970	1975
Black				
Total Men, 18 to 24 years	839	887	1,220	1,451
Total Enrolled in College	41	63	192	294
Percent of total	5	7	16	20
Total Women, 18 to 24 years	965	978	1,471	1,761
Total Enrolled in College	42	66	225	372
Percent of total	4	7	16	21
White				
Total Men, 18 to 24 years	6,856	6,888	9,053	11,050
Total Enrolled in College	1,025	1,267	3,096	3,326
Percent of total	15	19	34	30
Total Women, 18 to 24 years	7,118	6,921	10,555	11,653
Total Enrolled in College	558	811	2,209	2,790
Percent of total	8	12	21	24

*Data for "Black" include persons of "other" races.

SOURCE: Adapted from Table 66 in *The Social and Economic Status of the Black Population in the United States: An Historical View, 1790-1978*. Washington, D.C.: U.S. Department of Commerce, Bureau of the Census, Current Population Reports, Series P-23, No. 80.

As shown in Table 1, for black men between the ages of 18 and 24 years, the college enrollment rate in 1975 was 20 percent compared to only five percent in 1950. The college enrollment rate for black women was slightly higher at 21 percent in comparison to four percent in 1950. By contrast, the college enrollment rate for white men was 30 percent in 1975, which doubled the 15 percent observed in 1950. Only 8 percent of white women in the 18- to 24-year cohort enrolled in college in 1950; however, by 1975, the percent had reached 24 percent, which was still substantially lower than that for white men but higher than the rates for both black men and women in the same age cohorts.

At all levels of education, black Americans registered a more rapid rate of educational attainment than did white Americans. Such dramatic increases undoubtedly reflected the changing patterns of access throughout the nation stimulated by the Civil Rights Movement and enabling legislation enacted by the federal government consequent to the Brown decision in 1954. Simultaneous improvements were registered among white Americans, though not by the same rates. These rate differences also reflect the higher prevalence of access of white Americans to formal schooling at all levels. Consequently, due to lingering effects of historic patterns of exclusion, notwithstanding important changes in opportunity structure, it is still extremely difficult for blacks to close the education gap between themselves and whites in the United States. But the gap is closing.

Between 1950 and 1975, there was a 380 percent increase in the number of black males who had received four or more years of college. By contrast, white males registered a 210 percent increase for the same period. Among males who had received from one to three years of college education during that period, black males registered a 388 percent increase while the increase for white males was 140 percent. Dramatic increases were also revealed among black males who had completed four years of high school as well as for white males at the same level. The percent increases for black males and white males were 390 and 125, respectively. (Table 2).

TABLE 2

PERCENT CHANGE IN EDUCATIONAL ATTAINMENT BETWEEN 1950-1975, BY RACE AND SEX

	Percent Change by Race and Sex			
Years of Schooling	Black Males	White Males	Black Females	White Females
College—4 or more yrs.	380	210	315	177
College—1 to 3 yrs.	388	140	333	105
High School—4 yrs.	390	125	416	131

SOURCE: Adapted from "Years of School Completed By Americans," *The Chronicle of Higher Education*, September 13, 1976, p. 12.

Similar improvements in educational attainment at all levels were revealed for both black and white females. Among black females, the increases were 315 percent for four or more years of college, 333 for one to three years of college, and 416 percent for four years of high school. By contrast, the figures for white females were 177 percent, 105 percent, and 131 percent, respectively. (Table 2).

Such improvements in educational attainment continued throughout the 1970s. In 1980, the Census Bureau reported that, among all Americans 25 years and older, 21 percent had completed one or more years of college in 1970 but by 1979, more than 31 percent of them had achieved that level of education. The percent change for completion of four or more years of college was from 11 percent in 1970 to 16 percent in 1979 among all Americans 25 years of age or older (*The Chronicle*, October 20, 1980, p. 2).

Significantly, by 1979, almost one-half (49.4 percent) of all black Americans in the 25 years and older group had completed high school. This percent compared to 33.7 percent in 1970. In 1970, only 4.5 percent of blacks in this age group had completed four years of college. However, by 1979, the percent had risen to 7.9. Even with such dramatic change, blacks still lagged behind whites in college completion rates as evidenced by the 11.6 percent of whites who had completed four years of college in 1970 and the 17.2 percent college completion reported in 1979 (*The Chronicle*, October 20, 1980, p. 2).

Irrespective of race, women still lag behind men in college completion rates. For instance, in 1970, the college completion rates for white women and men 25 years and older were 8.6 percent and 15 percent, respectively, a difference of 6.4 percentage points between them. In 1979, these rates for white women and men were 13.3 percent and 21.4 percent, respectively, a difference of 8.1 percent between white men and women. In fact, despite the increases in the number of white women going to college, they lost ground in terms of the differences between themselves and white men in college completion rates. Clearly, blacks as a group lagged behind both white women and white men. However, the rates for black women were not significantly below those reported for black men in either 1970 or 1979. For instance, in 1970, 4.4 percent of black women and 4.6 percent of black men in this age cohort had completed four years of college, a difference of only 0.2 percent. In 1979, these figures were 7.5 percent and 8.3 percent, respectively, a difference of 0.8 percent. Once again, women had lost ground but the loss was less than one percentage point (*The Chronicle*, October 20, 1980, p. 2).

Among eighteen-year-olds in the general population, the 4,292,000 who enrolled in college for the first time in 1979 were the peak for that age population. It is expected that first-time college enrollees for persons of that age will continue to decline throughout this century. However, the enrollment decline for persons in the 18–24 age group is not anticipated until 1982 (Jack Magarrell, May 12, 1980). The number of black eighteen-year-olds, on the other hand, is not projected to decline as rapidly. Hence, this group and older blacks seeking a college education represent a significant pool for colleges and universities.

Although the number and proportions of black Americans who go to college and complete four or more years of college continue to increase, their underrepresentation in higher education remains a most serious problem. A significant part of that problem is explained by the exceptionally high dropout (and sometimes *pushout*) rate of blacks from high school. According to one source, there was a loss between ages 16 and 34 of some 7,255,000 blacks disqualified for college education in 1974 due to dropout from high school. In fact, the National Advisory Committee on Black Higher Education and Black Colleges and Universities reported in 1979 that in 1977 there were more black dropouts between the ages of 18 and 24 than there were black college enrollees that year. In fact, in 1977, 808,000 black persons or 24 percent of the 18- to 24-year-olds were not enrolled in school and they were not even high school graduates (National Advisory Committee, January, 1979).

In the 16–19 year age group, there is evidence that the black dropout rate has increased since 1977 and that the rate for this group approximates 15 percent of the age cohort. In general, blacks as a percent of total in this age cohort increased in college enrollment during the seventies but so has their dropout rate (National Advisory Committee, 1980). This loss of potential black college students has serious implications for the overall representation of blacks in higher education, the production of blacks with baccalaureate and advanced degrees, and for future available pools of black faculty.

Table 3 shows that the dropout rate for blacks in the 16–19 age cohort decreased between 1970 and 1977. However, it began to rise again in 1978 and has remained at approximately 15 percent. By contrast, the dropout rate for white males in this group increased in 1975 and continued to approximately 12.4 percent in 1979. Among 20- to 24-year-old blacks, the 1979 dropout rate was 26.6 percent of the total in the age group. Within the 25- to 34-year-old bracket, the dropout rate among blacks was only slightly lower in 1979 at 24.9 percent. The aggregate and real numbers of black persons in all these age groupings attest to the magnitude of the problem with respect to enrollment and graduation from college. (Table 3).

These data point to the magnitude and seriousness of the dropout problem among black students. This problem exists at

TABLE 3

BLACK AND WHITE DROPOUTS IN SELECTED AGE COHORTS 1970, 1975 TO 1979

Age cohort and race	1970	1975	1976	1977	1978	1979
16 - 19 Year Olds						
Black						
Total Population	1,855	2,167	2,207	2,235	2,234	2,229
Dropouts	399	378	320	324	343	338
Percent of total	21.5	17.4	14.5	14.5	15.4	15.2
White						
Total Population	12,642	13,898	13,968	13,976	13,906	13,825
Dropouts	1,330	1,599	1,718	1,725	1,720	1,710
Percent of total	10.5	11.5	12.3	12.3	12.4	12.4
20 - 24 Year Olds						
Black						
Total Population	1,814	2,183	2,260	2,315	2,387	2,438
Dropouts	623	615	592	573	592	649
Percent of total	34.3	28.2	26.2	24.8	24.8	26.6
White						
Total Population	13,599	15,848	16,168	16,486	16,717	16,915
Dropouts	2,129	2,144	2,276	2,342	2,382	2,456
Percent of total	15.7	13.5	14.1	14.2	14.2	14.5
25 - 34 Year Olds						
Black						
Total Population	2,669	3,186	3,315	3,455	3,586	3,752
Dropouts	1,149	1,018	936	958	905	933
Percent of total	43.0	32.0	28.2	27.7	25.2	24.9
White						
Total Population	21,691	26,571	27,473	28,291	28,943	29,844
Dropouts	4,773	4,268	4,436	4,169	4,017	4,002
Percent of total	22.0	16.1	16.1	14.7	13.9	13.4

SOURCE: U.S. Department of Commerce, Bureau of the Census, Series P-20.

SOURCE: Reprinted from *Target Date, 2000 A.D.: Goals for Achieving Higher Education Equity for Black Americans*. Washington, D.C.: National Advisory Committee on Black Higher Education, September 1980.

all levels of higher education. However, Alexander Astin's research shows that their highest dropout rates are in two-year institutions (Astin, 1975). The National Advisory Committee on Black Higher Education reported in 1979 that only 17 of 100 black freshmen persist to complete four years of college compared to 30 of every 100 white freshmen (National Advisory Committee, January 1979).

Income disabilities represent a major barrier to increasing the enrollment of black students in higher education. Despite income gains achieved by black Americans over the past thirty years, most evidence shows that the income gap between black and white families is widening. For instance, the median family income of black families in the United States fell from 61 percent of that of white families in 1969 to 59 percent in 1979. The decline in black family income proportionate to that of white families appears perpetual (Blackwell, 1981). Obviously, if blacks continue to experience an adult unemployment rate that approaches three times that of white adults and if the black teenage unemployment rate of 50.7 percent, acknowledged by the Reagan Administration but which is substantially higher in various cities, persists unabated, the impact on college attendance among blacks will be nothing short of devastating. Even now, there is substantial evidence that black undergraduate, graduate, and professional students come from families whose yearly income is less than $10,000 (Blackwell, 1981; Karabel, 1972; National Advisory Committee, 1979).

Elimination of such problems cannot be achieved without a major expansion of economic opportunity that facilitates greater equity in access to jobs, promotions and income, greater job security, and strengthening of financial aid programs. Further, as subsequent analyses will demonstrate, enrollment patterns among black students and improvements in the presence of black faculty and administrators will not occur without a rekindled commitment to that goal, unbiased counseling of exceptionally high quality, conscientious recruitment and monumental changes in the hiring and retention of black faculty.

Desegregation in Community Colleges

Two-year community colleges have played an immensely important role in facilitating greater access of black students to higher education. In fact, the increasing proportionate concentration of black students in two-year colleges often distorts overall enrollment data. For example, it could be misleading to point to the presence of in excess of 1,100,000 blacks in higher education in 1981 without a delineation of how that number is distributed in the various levels of higher education. Further, great differences exist between institutions according to their control (i.e., public vs. private), States in which they are located, their proximity to a fairly large black population, and the type of city in which they are found. There is some evidence to suggest also that the enrollment of black students in community colleges may be influenced by the litigation status of a given state with respect to the *Adams* v. *Califano/Bell* case. Among other factors that account for the concentration of large numbers of black students in two-year community colleges are their low tuition and open enrollment policies (Gail Thomas, 1981; National Advisory Committee on Black Higher Education and Black Colleges and Universities, January 1979).

The proportion of blacks enrolled in two-year community colleges climbed steadily throughout the 1970s. By the end of the decade, 50 percent of all blacks in higher education were enrolled in such institutions. At the same time, high concentrations were reported for other minority groups such as Hispanics with 59 percent of their numbers enrolled in two-year colleges, American Indians with a concentration of 67 percent, and Asian Americans, who enrolled 52 percent of their college students in two-year institutions. By contrast, less than one-half (45 percent) of all white students were enrolled at that level even though white students comprise seventy-nine percent of all community college enrollees (Institute for the Study of Educational Policy, 1980, 15). These percentages refer to both full- and part-time students.

The degree of concentration of black and other minority students in community colleges is more readily apparent when the full-time student and part-time cohorts are analyzed separately. The ISEP reports that while slightly more than one-fourth (27 percent) of all full-time white students are enrolled in community colleges, the concentration is substantially greater for minority groups. Specifically, one-third of full-time Asian students, almost two-fifths (37 percent) of black students, more than two-fifths (45 percent) of Hispanic students, and slightly less than one-half (48 percent) of all full-time American Indian students are enrolled in two-year community colleges (ISEP, 1980).

Earlier on, the explanations offered for this higher concentration of blacks in community colleges included open admissions policies, lower tuition than that demanded at most four-year colleges and universities, and proximity to urban areas in which blacks represent a sizeable proportion of the population. It is undoubtedly a consequence of the latter phenomenon that the lower number of "Newer Predominantly Black Colleges" (NPBCs) is increasing. It is estimated that the number of NPBCs increased by twenty-four institutions between 1976 and 1978 and these institutions were primarily two-year institutions. Unfortunately, many students who have the academic potential to pursue a strong academic curriculum, whether in NPBCs or in other community colleges, are channeled into vocational programs that all but preclude immediate transfer to upper-division universities, four-year colleges, and other universities (ISEP, 1980; Barron, 1973; Gleaser, 1973; and Brazziel, 1981).

Many community colleges with sizeable black student enrollment are located in states with substantially large black populations. Several are found in states presently under litigation to dismantle dual systems of higher education or under pressure to increase the presence of minority students in the higher education system. These states are often referred to as the "Adams States," in reference to court decisions rendered in the original *Adams* v. *Richardson* case in which ten states were ordered to dismantle dual systems of higher education and discontinue practices which restricted access of blacks to all levels of higher education. The state plans pertinent to this process, ordered by the court in the subsequent *Adams* v. *Califano* decisions, were also expected to demonstrate methods by which the various states would "enhance the historically black colleges" (Brazziel, 1981; Blackwell, 1981; and Pruitt, 1981). The original list of ten states was expanded to nineteen during the lame duck period of the Carter Administration under pressure from the NAACP-LDF and with the concurrence of the Justice Department.

Tables 4 and 5 present enrollment data by state, college type/control, race and percent for 1976. The states included are states which theoretically and/or by litigation are encompassed by the "Adams" mandates. At this juncture, specific attention is called only to enrollment in two-year colleges. These tables show that in 1976, 36.7 percent of all black students were enrolled in two-year institutions. Sharp differences between states in the

TABLE 4

ENROLLMENT OF BLACK STTDENTS IN ADAMS-CALIFANO STATES BY COLLEGE TYPE: PUBLIC AND PRIVATE INSTITUTIONS 1976

ALL FIELDS

		Black		White	
State	All	2-Year	4-Year	2-Year	4-Year
Totals	**452,795**	**8,396**	**149,651**	**157,792**	**136,956**
Alabama	28,381	1,315	13,840	6,754	6,472
Arkansas	8,967	189	2,971	917	4,890
Delaware	2,425	—	1,183	631	611
Florida	34,626	—	6,120	20,897	7,609
Georgia	24,411	—	12,463	4,650	7,298
Kentucky	8,391	—	1,284	2,321	4,786
Louisiana	32,022	973	16,992	3,707	10,350
Maryland	31,329	—	8,395	15,912	7,022
Mississippi	24,951	3,127	13,137	5,183	3,504
Missouri	15,227	—	821	6,919	7,487
North Carolina	42,003	2,063	19,438	15,272	5,230
Ohio	39,376	—	2,768	15,488	21,120
Oklahoma	8,409	—	989	3,518	3,902
Pennsylvania	25,321	—	2,939	9,750	12,632
South Carolina	22,354	—	7,892	9,860	4,602
Tennessee	22,715	173	7,881	6,474	8,187
Texas	53,043	317	14,643	23,401	15,682
Virginia	25,819	239	15,114	6,756	3,710
West Virginia	3,025	—	781	382	1,862

NOTE: An additional 6,217 students were enrolled in colleges uncoded by race.

SOURCE: Reprinted from William and Marian Brazziel, *Recent College and University Enrollment Patterns of Black Students in States Affected By Adams-Califano Litigation.* Atlanta: Southern Education Foundation, 1981.

proportion of black students enrolled in these institutions are also apparent in these tables, especially Table 5. For instance, at one extreme is Florida, which enrolled 60.3 percent of its black students in two-year colleges. At the opposite end of the spectrum is Arkansas, in which 12.3 percent of blacks matriculated at these institutions. Both Florida and Arkansas were included in the original ten "Adams States." However, Florida has a much more extensive system of community colleges, than does Arkansas. West Virginia, on the other hand, which enrolls 12.6 percent of its black students in community colleges was not included in the original group of "Adams States." Two former historically black colleges, West Virginia State College and Bluefield State

TABLE 5

PERCENT OF BLACK STUDENTS ENROLLED IN TWO- AND FOUR-YEAR COLLEGES IN ADAMS-CALIFANO STATES IN 1976

State	All	Percent 2-Year	Percent 4-Year
Totals	**452,795**	**36.70**	**63.30**
Alabama	28,381	28.43	71.57
Arkansas	8,967	12.33	87.67
Delaware	2,425	26.02	73.98
Florida	34,626	60.35	39.65
Georgia	24,411	19.05	80.95
Kentucky	8,391	27.66	72.34
Louisiana	32,022	14.61	85.39
Maryland	31,329	50.79	49.21
Mississippi	24,951	33.31	66.69
Missouri	15,227	45.44	54.56
North Carolina	42,003	41.27	58.73
Ohio	39,376	39.33	60.67
Oklahoma	8,409	41.84	58.16
Pennsylvania	25,321	38.51	61.49
South Carolina	22,354	44.11	55.89
Tennessee	22,715	29.26	70.74
Texas	53,043	42.83	57.17
Virginia	25,819	27.09	72.91
West Virginia	3,025	12.63	87.37

SOURCE: Reprinted from William and Marian Brazziel, *Recent College and University Enrollment Black Students in States Affected By Adams-Califano Litigation.* Atlanta: Southern Education Foundation, 1981.

College, are seldom currently classified as HBCs because of the majority or near majority of white students enrolled when headcounts are employed as the measure of total enrollment.

The highest percents of black student enrollment in public and private two-year institutions among these nineteen states in 1976 were found, in descending order, in: Florida, Maryland, Missouri, South Carolina, Texas, and Oklahoma. Not unexpectedly, these states rank last with respect to the proportion of blacks enrolled in four-year colleges.

William Brazziel reported that the nineteen states encompassed by the *Adams* decision had a total population of approximately 90 million people. Almost seventeen (16.7) percent of that population were black. He also found that of the three million undergraduates in these states, only 13.8 percent were black students. Hence, black students are underrepresented with respect to the population as a whole; they are also slightly below the 14 percent which blacks comprise of the 18–22 college age population (Brazziel, 1981, 23).

The data provided in Table 4 also permit comparisons among black and white two-year colleges within the various states. Black two-year colleges were present in 1976 in only eight states: Alabama, Arkansas, Louisiana, Mississippi, North Carolina, Tennessee, Texas, and Virginia. Among these states, Mississippi, North Carolina, and Alabama enrolled larger numbers of blacks in two-year black colleges. However, more than five times the number of black junior college students were enrolled in the white junior colleges in Alabama than the number enrolled in institutions characterized as black. Substantially greater ratios than 5:1 observed in Alabama were apparent in such states as North Carolina, Tennessee, Texas, and Virginia (Table 4).

In 1976, several of the 19 states enrolled more black students in the two-year institutions classified as "white" than they did in the white four-year colleges. These states included Alabama, Florida, Maryland, Mississippi, North Carolina, South Carolina, Texas, and Virginia (Table 4). In fact, there were more blacks enrolled in 1976 in the white two-year colleges in Florida, Kentucky, Maryland, Missouri, Ohio, Pennsylvania, and Texas than were black students enrolled in the historically black institutions within these states (Table 4).

A brief examination of Table 6 shows that in 1976, most black junior college students were enrolled in colleges under public control. This observation held whether one considered black or white colleges. Undoubtedly, this pattern could be attributed to both low tuition costs and convenient locations. That finding is not particularly unique. What is noteworthy is the distinction in enrollment patterns observed for white institutions. For instance, such states as Alabama, Oklahoma, and Tennessee about equally distributed black students enrolled in white public institutions. However, the same was not the case for such states as Florida, Maryland, North Carolina, Mississippi, South Carolina, Texas, and Virginia. In each of these states, black students matriculated in white, public institutions were far more likely than not to be found in the two-year colleges than in four-year institutions (Table 6).

TABLE 6

ENROLLMENT OF BLACK STUDENTS IN ADAMS-CALIFANO STATES BY COLLEGE TYPE: PUBLIC INSTITUTIONS 1976

ALL FIELDS

		Black		White	
State	All	2-Year	4-Year	2-Year	4-Year
Totals	**368,326**	**6,703**	**103,708**	**150,822**	**107,093**
Alabama	19,196	1,315	5,933	5,983	5,965
Arkansas	7,529	—	2,521	881	4,127
Delaware	1,925	—	1,183	303	439
Florida	29,815	—	4,375	20,886	4,554
Georgia	16,477	—	5,822	4,243	6,412
Kentucky	7,680	—	1,284	2,213	4,183
Louisiana	28,589	973	14,289	3,707	9,620
Maryland	29,607	—	8,395	14,893	6,319
Mississippi	22,027	2,352	11,381	5,155	3,139
Missouri	12,146	—	821	6,863	4,462
North Carolina	33,080	2,063	13,176	14,263	3,578
Ohio	31,812	—	1,699	14,706	15,407
Oklahoma	7,673	—	989	3,261	3,423
Pennsylvania	19,198	—	2,939	8,974	7,285
South Carolina	15,718	—	2,894	9,136	3,688
Tennessee	17,291	—	4,091	6,292	6,908
Texas	17,291	—	10,379	22,307	12,980
West Virginia	2,577	—	781	247	1,549

SOURCE: Reprinted from William and Marian Brazziel, *Recent College and University Enrollment Patterns of Black Students in States Affected By Adams-Califano Litigation.* Atlanta: Southern Education Foundation, 1981.

An examination of Tables 7, 8, and 9 reveals a similar pattern in the distribution of black students between two-year and four-year institutions in these 19 states. By 1978, 38.8 percent of all black college students were located in the two-year colleges within the "Adams States," and 61.1 percent were enrolled in their four-year colleges and universities. Again, greater concentrations of blacks in junior colleges were recorded for Florida, Maryland, South Carolina, North Carolina, Texas, and Missouri. On the whole, more than twice as many blacks were enrolled in the white two-year colleges (118,170) than in the black two-year colleges (47,539).

Again, substantially larger numbers of black students were enrolled in the white two-year colleges than in similar black institutions in several states. These states included all states except Missouri, Oklahoma and Pennsylvania. Florida stood out for the exceptionally high proportion of its black students enrolled in white community colleges in relation to black student enrollment in either the historically black public institutions or the historically white institutions (Tables 7, 8 and 9).

TABLE 7

PERCENT OF BLACK STUDENTS ENROLLED IN TWO- AND FOUR-YEAR COLLEGES IN ADAMS-CALIFANO STATES IN 1978

State	All	Percent 2-Year	Percent 4-Year
Totals	**474,992**	**38.85**	**61.15**
Alabama	32,007	33.86	66.14
Arkansas	9,891	19.98	80.02
Delaware	3,064	40.21	59.79
Florida	35,529	57,78	42.22
Georgia	27,223	24.01	75.99
Kentucky	7,890	28.75	71.25
Louisiana	32,655	13.97	86.03
Maryland	31,962	51.91	48.09
Mississippi	25,473	36.78	63.22
Missouri	14,992	44.46	55.54
North Carolina	46,893	45.82	54.18
Ohio	36,108	38.46	61.54
Oklahoma	8,205	40.87	59.13
Pennsylvania	28,886	40.36	59.64
South Carolina	25,249	48.59	51.41
Tennessee	25,545	34.01	65.99
Texas	54,021	45.47	54.53
Virginia	26,609	29.00	71.00
West Virginia	2,790	12.97	87.03

SOURCE: Reprinted from William and Marian Brazziel, *Recent College And University Enrollment Patterns of Black Students in States Affected By Adams-Califano Litigation*. Atlanta: Southern Education Foundation, 1981.

As recent as 1979, Astin and Cross observed that one-third of all black full-time freshmen were enrolled in the predominantly black public institutions, disproportionately in community colleges. However, only 13 percent of the most able black students, as measured by performance on the Scholastic Aptitude Test (SAT) were enrolled in black institutions (Astin and Sherrei, 1979).

TABLE 8

ENROLLMENT OF BLACK STUDENTS IN ADAMS-CALIFANO STATES BY COLLEGE TYPE: PUBLIC AND PRIVATE INSTITUTIONS 1978

ALL FIELDS

		Black		White		Other	
State	All	2-Year	4-Year	2-Year	4-Year	2-Year	4-Year
Totals	**474,992**	**47,539**	**144,497**	**118,170**	**142,797**	**18,846**	**3,143**
Alabama	32,007	2,830	13,229	6,455	7,937	1,554	2
Arkansas	9,891	169	2,893	1,119	4,506	688	516
Delaware	3,064	—	1,177	807	655	425	—
Florida	35,529	4,855	7,488	15,585	7,401	90	110
Georgia	27,223	1,526	12,166	4,550	8,521	460	—
Kentucky	7,890	—	1,194	1,880	4,428	388	—
Louisiana	32,655	688	17,677	3,812	10,416	62	—
Maryland	31,962	6,436	7,867	9,977	7,432	180	70
Mississippi	25,473	3,401	12,603	5,193	3,500	776	—
Missouri	14,992	3,742	755	2,924	6,763	—	808
N. Carolina	46,893	3,146	18,836	16,417	6,565	1,925	4
Ohio	36,108	5,474	3,019	8,409	19,202	3	1
Oklahoma	8,205	5,474	847	3,304	4,005	49	—
Pennsylvania	28,886	7,747	3,602	3,853	13,578	58	48
S. Carolina	25,249	2,220	7,291	8,065	5,689	1,984	—
Tennessee	25,545	2,897	7,314	4,302	9,542	1,490	—
Texas	54,021	2,042	12,810	13,805	15,066	8,714	1,584
Virginia	26,609	366	13,729	7,351	5,163	—	—
W. Virginia	2,790	—	—	362	2,428	—	—

SOURCE: Reprinted from William and Marian Brazziel, *Recent Colleges and University Enrollment Patterns of Black Students in States Affected by Adams-Califano Litigation*. Atlanta: Southern Education Foundation, 1981.

The Special Case of Blacks in Florida

Florida's three-tier system of higher education exemplified some of the major issues involved in discussions of distribution of black students in higher education. Such issues include those of concentration, access and transferability to four-year colleges and universities, dropout or attrition rates from college, and graduation rates.

As indicated in Table 10, black college students in Florida are heavily concentrated in community colleges. In 1970, blacks comprised 9.1 percent of all students enrolled at three levels of higher education and 8.9 percent of all community college stu-

TABLE 9

ENROLLMENT OF BLACK STUDENTS IN ADAMS-CALIFANO STATES BY COLLEGE TYPE: PUBLIC INSTITUTIONS 1978

ALL FIELDS

		Black		White		Other	
State	All	2-Year	4-Year	2-Year	4-Year	2-Year	4-Year
Totals	**382,825**	**44,064**	**100,621**	**112,897**	**111,322**	**11,630**	**2,291**
Alabama	22,006	2,434	6,296	5,859	7,417	—	—
Arkansas	8,177	—	2,504	1,105	4,220	348	—
Delaware	2,656	—	1,177	615	439	425	—
Florida	29,935	4,855	4,666	15,559	4,855	—	—
Georgia	17,806	1,401	5,034	3,808	7,563	—	—
Kentucky	6,566	—	1,192	1,549	3,825	—	—
Louisiana	29,043	688	14,888	3,812	9,655	—	—
Maryland	30,867	6,436	7,867	9,919	6,477	168	—
Mississippi	21,916	2,216	10,904	5,155	3,052	589	—
Missouri	11,841	3,731	648	2,905	3,750	—	807
N. Carolina	36,149	2,662	12,703	15,861	4,588	335	—
Ohio	28,361	5,474	1,883	7,404	13,600	—	—
Oklahoma	7,549	—	847	3,218	3,484	—	—
Pennsylvania	22,425	7,747	3,602	3,101	7,917	58	—
S. Carolina	17,468	1,851	2,872	7,695	4,207	843	—
Tennessee	18,856	2,748	3,732	4,144	8,082	150	—
Texas	47,507	1,697	9,381	13,779	12,452	8,714	1,494
Virginia	21,349	124	9,644	7,214	4,367	—	—
W. Virginia	2,348	—	781	195	1,372	—	—

SOURCE: Reprinted from William and Marian Brazziel, *Recent Colleges and University Enrollment Patterns of Black Students in States Affected by Adams-Califano Litigation.* Atlanta: Southern Education Foundation, 1981.

dents, but 54.2 percent of them were enrolled in community colleges. As the proportion of blacks in the statewide profile increased, so was there an apparent increase in the proportion of blacks enrolled in community colleges. For instance, by 1976, black students comprised 15.1 percent of full-time enrollment in the statewide system. However, 61.9 percent of all black students were enrolled in the state's community colleges. This trend is further borne out by findings which include full-and-part-time students. During 1977, for instance, the aggregate of full- and part-time black students represented 14.1 percent of total statewide college student enrollment. In 1970, the rates were 13.6 percent of total statewide enrollment and 67.6 percent community college enrollment (Table 10).

TABLE 10

BLACK PARTICIPATION IN FLORIDA'S PUBLIC HIGHER EDUCATION ENROLLMENT TRENDS

	FALL 1970[1]				FALL 1974[1]				FALL 1976[1]			
	Black		White		Black		White		Black		White	
	Number	Percent	Number	Percent	Number	Percent	Number	Percent	Number	Percent	Number	Percent
State Wide	10,378	9.1	103,741	90.9	14,550	10.9	118,770	89.1	20,596	15.1	115,685	84.9
Trad. Blk. Inst.	3,841	98.5	58	1.5	3,545	95.5	168	4.5	4,132	91.6	381	8.4
S.U.S.TWI	913	1.9	46,434	98.1	2,754	4.6	57,056	95.4	3,715	6.0	54,813	94.0
2-Year Colleges	5,624	8.9	57,247	91.1	8,250	11.3	61,546	88.2	12,750	17.4	60,491	82.6
Percent of State Wide Totals												
Fl. A&M	37.0		.0		24.4		.0		20.1		.0	
SUS(TWI)	8.8		44.8		18.9		48.1		18.0		47.4	
2-Year Colleges	54.2		55.2		56.7		51.8		61.9		52.3	

	FALL 1976[2]				FALL 1977[2]				FALL 1978[2]			
	Black		White		Black		White		Black		White	
	Number	Percent	Number	Percent	Number	Percent	Number	Percent	Number	Percent	Number	Percent
State Wide	32,006	13.6	203,129	86.4	33,505	14.1	204,943	85.9	31,442	13.0	210,450	87.0
Trad. Blk. Inst.	4,842	87.7	678	12.3	4,777	90.4	508	9.6	4,647	91.8	410	8.2
S.U.S.TWI	5,516	6.6	78,695	93.4	5,746	6.9	78,059	93.1	6,381	7.2	82,301	92.8
2-Year Colleges	21,648	14.9	123,756	85.1	22,982	15.4	126,376	84.6	20,414	13.8	127,739	86.2
Percent of State Wide Totals												
Fl. A&M	15.1		.0		14.2		.1		14.7		.0	
SUS(TWI)	17.2		38.8		17.1		38.1		20.3		39.1	
2-Year Colleges	67.6		61.1		68.6		61.6		64.9		60.8	

1. Full Time Enrollment
2. Full and Part-time Enrollment

SOURCE: Reprinted from Charles Grigg, *Access Retention and Progression of Black Students Through the Two-Tier Florida Higher Education System*. Atlanta: Southern Education Foundation, 1981.

Except for 1970, a greater proportion of blacks than whites were enrolled in Florida's community colleges. The percent of white students enrolled in community colleges in 1970 was 55.2 compared to 54.2 for blacks that year. In all subsequent years, the percent black of black college students enrolled in community colleges has been higher than the percent white enrolled in similar institutions among all white college students (Table 10).

Black students in community colleges are also concentrated in about five of the 28 institutions which comprise the community college system. These colleges are located in the larger urban areas and near the population centers in which the majority of the black population lives. They include Florida Junior College, Miami Dade, Palm Beach, Santa Fe, Valencia, and Hillsborough (Grigg, 1981).

In 1977, 22,982 black students were enrolled in the 28 community colleges. This figure represented a 6.2 percent increase over the 1976 figure. By contrast, the percent increase for the same time period among white students in community colleges was only 2.4 percent. In 1978, black community college enrollment showed a decline of approximately 11.2 percent or down to 22,414. White enrollment increased by one percent in 1978. However, this reduction in the number of black community college students depressed overall statewide representation to 12.6 percent of total enrollment (Grigg, 1981).

Progression rates: Charles Grigg's analysis of progression rates of black students from community colleges into the upper-division universities and four-year colleges and universities revealed striking inequities between the races. In general, the majority (56.0 percent) of community college Associated Arts degree (A.A.) graduates in Florida do not move into advanced degree programs. However, 45 percent of "whites and others," in comparison to 35.1 percent of blacks do make a successful transition to four-year institutions if they have the A.A. degree. Proportionately, more black men (39.8 percent) than black women (32.2 percent) move on into the four-year colleges or universities. In either case, there is a significant loss of students for higher levels of education because of this failure to make the transfer to upper division, four-year colleges and universities (Grigg, 1981).

Erroneous conclusions may be drawn concerning the presence of black students in the higher educational statewide system. For instance, the 11.8 percent black student representation in the state university system reported for 1978 was inflated by the presence of historically black Florida A & M University in the data. Grigg's analysis revealed that blacks comprised only 6.4 percent of students in the traditionally white institutions (TWIs) and 9.8 percent of all students in the white upper-division universities (Grigg, 1981). Brazziel's study suggests similar patterns appear to exist in several additional states such as Maryland, North Carolina, Texas, and South Carolina.

Desegregation of Four-Year Colleges and Universities

Historical Overview: Without question, black students today have greater access to higher education than at any previous time in American history. However, formidable barriers remain which prevent full and equal participation in higher education. Although optimists may wish to treat de jure and de facto discrimination and segregation as past history, there is some evidence that many institutions throughout the United States remain essentially racially separate and segregated. This situation may be the result of any number of factors such as restrictive admissions policies, uninterest in the recruitment and selection of black and other minority students, economic barriers which prevent academically able minority students from enrolling in predominantly white schools when and if they are accepted, weak academic preparation in high schools and community colleges which disqualify such students from acceptance into four-year colleges and universities, and other factors.

Black and white young people are considerably more likely to be enrolled in college today than they were thirty years ago. The unique characteristic of black student enrollment is that their matriculation today is more often than not in colleges and universities that would have excluded them because of either de jure or de facto policies. For instance, in 1952–53, the combined enrollment of black students in twenty-two historically white public institutions was 253 in the South (Johnson, 1954). In the same year, the historically black colleges, most of which were located in the South, enrolled 63,000 black students (Mingle, 1978). The litigation initiated during the 1930s and 1940s by the NAACP and the Legal Defense and Educational Fund continued thereafter with the result that an increasing number of public institutions admitted black students.

Despite court orders, Mingle estimates that as late as 1960, when the Civil Rights Movement's activity escalated, the historically black institutions in the South enrolled about 96 percent of all black college students in the South. Significantly, between 1952 and 1960, the number of blacks enrolled in the historically white institutions had risen to 3,000. A year later, only seventeen percent of the traditionally white institutions of the South would admit black students. Primarily due to relentless pressure to force compliance with court orders, an increasing number of Southern colleges and universities enrolled greater numbers of black students. Consequently, by 1965, 24,000 black students were enrolled in traditionally white institutions located in the South (Mingle, 1978).

The dramatic increases in black student presence at the traditionally white institutions impacted negatively on the historically black colleges and universities located in the same state. This situation may be illustrated by the following observations. For instance, between 1965 and 1970, black student enrollment in the South increased by a phenomenal 83 percent or from 134,000 to 245,000. That trend continued so that the percentage of black student enrollment in predominantly and historically black institutions fell from 82 percent in 1970 to 43 percent in 1976 (Mingle, 1978). According to the National Center for Education Statistics, of the 1,106,321 black students enrolled in colleges in 1980–81, 55 percent are inside Southern/border states and 45 percent are outside these areas. Fifty-nine (59) percent of the 403,800 enrolled in black colleges are in four-year institutions.

As black student college enrollment increases, there appears to be a simultaneous rise in the number of newer predominantly black institutions (NPBIs). The National Advisory Committee on Black Higher Education and Black Colleges and Universities defines NPBIs as recently established institutions in close proximity to the black population of a given area and which have become predominantly black. In 1976, there were forty-two institutions so classified (National Advisory Committee, 1979, 13).

Status of Participation: The participation of black students in four-year institutions may be demonstrated by an analysis of 1976 and 1978 data which described special features of black students in the nineteen "Adams States." Black students were enrolled in 1,335 institutions in the "Adams States" in 1976 and these 1,335 institutions represented 44 percent of the nation's 3,055 colleges and universities. In that year, there were 459,012 black undergraduate students enrolled in the 120 historically and newer predominantly black institutions and in the 1,215 traditionally white institutions. This enrollment represented 13.8 percent of the 3,270,378 students enrolled in the 19 states. However, blacks comprised 16.7 percent of the total population of the 19 states. The almost half-million black students of the 19 states constituted 43 percent of the 1,034,680 black college students for the nation as a whole (Brazziel, 1981). One caveat must be made at this juncture: the figures cited include *all* undergraduate enrollment, junior and senior colleges, and four-year institutions.

As shown in Table 11, of the 452,795 black students enrolled in institutions coded by race, 63.3 percent or 286,607 were enrolled in four-year institutions. Of this number, 149,651 (33.1 percent) were studying at four-year black colleges and 136,956 (30.2 percent) were studying at four-year institutions. In general, states with less extensive two-year college systems enrolled more black students in four-year colleges. This observation is borne out by the higher proportions of blacks in four-year colleges in Arkansas (87.7 percent), West Virginia (87.4 percent), Louisiana (85.4 percent), and Georgia (80.9 percent). On the other hand, some states either channeled proportionately more black students into two-year institutions or black students purposely selected these institutions for special reasons. Consequently, black student enrollment in four-year institutions was comparatively low. Examples include Florida (39.7 percent), Maryland (49.2 percent), Missouri (54.6 percent), South Carolina (55.9 percent), Texas (57.2 percent), Oklahoma (58.2 percent), and North Carolina (58.7 percent).

In the following states, the percentage of black students matriculated in black colleges was higher than that for black students enrolled in white colleges in the same state in 1976: Alabama, Delaware, Georgia, Louisiana, Maryland, North Carolina, South Carolina, and Virginia. The remaining nine states had fewer historically black colleges located in them than in the group of states mentioned immediately above. In all nineteen states, the role of the historically black colleges should be apparent. Were it not for their presence, at least one-third of all black students then rolled in four-year institutions would have been forced to make alternative arrangements for their college education (Table 11).

Table 11 also shows that more black students were enrolled in the four-year colleges in Texas, Louisiana, North Carolina, Ohio, and Alabama than in the remainder of the nineteen States.

TABLE 11

FOUR YEAR COLLEGE STUDENT DISTRIBUTION, BY TYPE OF INSTITUTION, 1976

State	Total Enrollment	Black 4-Year	% of Total Enrollment	White 4-Year	% of Total Enrollment	Total 4-Year	% of Total Enrollment
All	452,795	149,651	33.1	136,956	30.2	286,607	63.2
Alabama	28,381	13,840	48.8	6,472	22.8	20,312	71.6
Arkansas	8,967	2,971	33.1	4,890	54.5	7,861	87.7
Delaware	2,425	1,183	48.8	611	25.2	1,794	74.0
Florida	34,626	6,120	17.7	7,609	22.0	13,729	39.7
Georgia	24,411	12,463	51.0	7,298	29.9	19,761	80.9
Kentucky	8,391	1,284	15.3	4,786	57.0	6,070	72.3
Louisiana	32,022	16,992	53.1	10,350	32.3	27,342	85.4
Maryland	31,329	8,395	26.8	7,022	22.4	15,417	49.2
Mississippi	24,951	13,137	52.7	3,504	14.0	16,641	66.7
Missouri	15,227	821	5.4	7,487	49.2	8,308	54.6
North Carolina	42,003	19,438	46.3	5,230	12.5	24,668	58.7
Ohio	39,376	2,768	7.0	21,120	53.6	23,888	60.7
Oklahoma	8,409	989	11.8	3,902	46.4	4,891	58.2
Pennsylvania	25,321	2,939	11.6	12,632	49.9	15,571	61.5
South Carolina	22,354	7,892	35.3	4,602	20.6	12,494	55.9
Tennessee	22,715	7,881	34.7	8,187	36.0	16,068	70.7
Texas	53,043	14,643	27.6	15,682	29.6	30,325	57.2
Virginia	25,819	15,114	58.5	3,710	14.4	18,824	72.9
West Virginia	3,025	781	25.8	1,862	61.6	2,643	87.4

SOURCE: Reprinted from William Brazziel and Marian Brazziel, *Recent College and University Enrollment Patterns of Black Students in States Affected by Adams-Califano Litigation*. Atlanta: Southern Education Foundation, 1981.

However, when the percent of blacks in the total state population was measured against total enrollment, the six leading states in enrolling blacks in 1976 were West Virginia (4.7 percent), Oklahoma (4.4 percent), Ohio and Maryland (each with 3.8 percent), and North Carolina, Tennessee, and Texas (each with 3.5 percent) (Brazziel, 1981). The percent of blacks in the population for each of the states cited in this paragraph is listed in Table 12.

TABLE 12

PERCENT OF BLACKS IN STATE POPULATION OF SELECTED STATES, 1976

States	% Black in Population	States	% Black in Population
Alabama	27	Oklahoma	7
Louisiana	31	Tennessee	17
Maryland	21	Texas	14
North Carolina	23	West Virginia	4
Ohio	10		

1978 Comparisons: In the 1978 Fall Semester, a total of 11,260,092 students enrolled in undergraduate schools throughout the nation. The full-time enrollment for black men was 285,008 while that for black women was 369,219. Part-time black student enrollment was 168,248 for men and 231,896 for women.

National enrollment figures for all students in terms of institutional control were distributed as follows in the Fall of 1978: 8,785,893 in public institutions; 2,474,199 in private institutions. Four-year public universities accounted for 2,062,295 while four-year private universities enrolled 718,434 students. Four-year public colleges enrolled 2,849,908 and four-year private colleges enrolled 1,601,314 students. In total, four-year universities accounted for 2,780,729 while four-year colleges enrolled 4,451,222 students in 1978 (National Center for Education Statistics, 1980).

The nineteen "Adams States" enrolled 474,992 students at all levels of higher education in the Fall of 1978. This number was distributed as follows: 47,539 in two-year black colleges, 118,170 in two-year white colleges, 144,497 in four-year black institutions, and 142,797 in white four-year institutions. The remaining 22,000 students were distributed in "other" two- and four-year institutions (Table 8).

With respect to four-year institutions, more black students in these 19 states were enrolled in black colleges and universities than in white four-year institutions. In fact, significantly more black students were enrolled in the black colleges than in white institutions of the following states: Alabama, Delaware, Georgia, Louisiana, Mississippi, North Carolina, South Carolina, and Virginia. On the other hand, significantly larger numbers of black students were enrolled in the white four-year institutions of this set of states: Arkansas, Kentucky, Missouri, Ohio, Oklahoma, Pennsylvania, Tennessee, and Texas (Table 8).

Although these nineteen states showed a 3.9 percent gain between 1976 and 1978 in the number of black students enrolled in higher education, this gain was primarily seen in enrollment changes in the newer predominantly black two-year institutions. All states, with the exception of Kentucky, Ohio, Oklahoma, and West Virginia, which experienced enrollment declines among black students, showed from modest (1.84 percent in Texas) to significant percentage gains in black student enrollment (e.g., 12.85 percent gain in South Carolina) (Brazziel, 1981).

Enrollment by Control: Among public, four-year institutions, 100,621 black students were matriculated at the four-year black colleges and universities and 111,322 were enrolled in the white institutions. The black-white institution distribution pattern of higher black student concentration in the black public institutions of some states and higher enrollment in the white public institutions of a smaller number observed in 1976 continued in 1978. For instance, there was a significantly higher concentration of black students in the black four-year public institutions in the following states: Louisiana, Mississippi, North Carolina, and Virginia. On the other hand, black students were more likely to be enrolled in the white institutions of such states as Arkansas, Missouri, Ohio, Oklahoma, Pennsylvania, South Carolina, Tennessee, and Texas. Given the existence of only a single public predominantly black college in most of these states, this finding may not be unexpected (Table 9). It is illuminating nonetheless.

In 1978, only 30,694 black students were enrolled in the predominantly white private four-year institutions of the nineteen states. The 44,657 black students enrolled in the private four-year institutions accounted for slightly under 50 percent of the 92,167 black students enrolled at all levels in the private colleges (Brazziel, 1981, 39).

Enrollment by Fields: As shown in Table 13, the Business and Management majors are far more attractive to black students

TABLE 13

ENROLLMENT OF BLACK STUDENTS IN ADAMS-CALIFANO STATES BY FIELD AND COLLEGE TYPE

Field	Total Enrollees	Percent by Type					
		Black		White		Other	
		2-Year	4-Year	2-Year	4-Year	2-Year	4-Year
Total	**470,786**	**10.10**	**29.80**	**25.10**	**30.33**	**4.00**	**.67**
Agriculture	1,899	.11	69.46	6.74	21.70	—	2.00
Architecture	1,501	5.66	47.63	6.40	39.71	—	.60
Biological Science	11,324	2.19	53.81	4.47	37.62	1.03	.88
Business &	82,044	6.07	33.98	16.39	33.19	9.36	1.02
Engineering	12,653	3.16	32.45	12.94	49.31	1.38	.76
Physical Sciences	3,994	2.98	49.35	7.46	35.38	4.11	.73
All Others	357,371	11.67	27.48	28.56	28.72	3.00	.57

	Summary of Gains and Losses 1976	1978	
Agriculture	1,796	1,899	+103
Architecture	988	1,501	+513
Biological Sciences	11,824	11,324	−550
Business & Management	70,128	82,044	+11,816
Engineering	10,763	12,653	+ 1,890
Physical Sciences	3,815	3,994	−179

SOURCE: Reprinted from William and Marian Brazziel, *Recent College and University Enrollment Patterns of Black Students in States Affected by Adams-Califano Litigation.* Atlanta: Southern Education Foundation, 1981.

than all others. The second and third concentration of majors are in Engineering and the Biological Sciences. The fourth position, with respect to major fields of black college students, is that of the Physical Sciences, which is followed by Architecture. Although black student enrollment in such fields as Agriculture increased slightly, the black schools of agriculture feel that enrollment could have been much more substantial had their institutions been given equal resources to their white counterparts among the land-grant institutions in these states. Because of federal government neglect and underfunding of black institutions and the relocation of majors in Natural Resources from black land-grant institutions to white land-grant colleges and universities in the same state (e.g., from South Carolina State College Orangeburg to Clemson), black schools of agriculture have not been able to continue their growth nor make comparable improvements of facilities and programs as have the white institutions (Lorenzo Middleton, 1979).

On the other hand, black undergraduate student interest in the field of Engineering has expanded by gigantic leaps within the past decade. The absolute numbers of black students enrolled in the nation's 282 colleges of Engineering rose from 2,757 or 1.3 percent of a total enrollment of 210,825 in 1969–70 to 12,786 or 4.3 percent of a total enrollment of 340,488 in 1979–80 (Table 14). This increase in the representation of blacks in Engineering resulted from aggressive recruitment efforts and direct involvement of private organizations in assisting Engineering colleges in the recruitment, enrollment, financial support, and training of black students in this field (Blackwell, 1981).

Prior to the 1970s, the six Colleges of Engineering located at historically black institutions* assumed the major responsibility for the training of black students in this field. Their role was especially critical prior to court-ordered desegregation with respect to the *Adams* case. Their value in the production of black engineers is underscored by the fact that between 1969 and 1973, these six institutions awarded almost one-half (47 percent) of all first professional degrees in Engineering received by black students. In 1969, they awarded 93 percent of all Engineering degrees earned by black students. This percent had not declined significantly by 1979. Hence, the six Engineering colleges located at historically black colleges today award a substantial number of first professional degrees to black students (Blackwell, 1981).

Among the original ten "Adams States," Mississippi has the highest percent (6.8 percent) black student enrollment in its Schools of Engineering. That state is followed in order by Maryland (5.2 percent), Pennsylvania and Virginia (4.7 percent), Georgia (4.6 percent), Florida (4.1 percent), Oklahoma (2.9 percent), Arkansas and North Carolina (2.4 percent), and Louisiana with 2.1 percent black student enrollment of all students enrolled in its Colleges of Engineering.

As shown in Table 15, the absolute number of B.S. degrees in engineering earned by black students more than doubled between 1970 and 1979. Over 900 blacks are currently being graduated each year with the B.S. degree in Engineering. However, a

*The six Colleges of Engineering are located at Howard University, North Carolina A & T University, Prairie View A & M University, Southern University, Tennessee State University, and Tuskegee Institute.

TABLE 14

FULL-TIME B. S. IN ENGINEERING ENROLLMENT PROGRAMS BY RACE, PERCENT OF TOTAL AND BY YEAR, 1969-79—ALL INSTITUTIONS COMBINED

Year	Total Enrollment	Total Black Students	Percent Black of Total
1969-70	210,825	2,757	1.3
1970-71	194,727	4,136	2.0
1971-72	186,705	4,356	2.2
1972-73	201,099	5,508	3.0
1973-74	186,700	5,508	3.0
1974-75	201,100	6,827	3.4
1975-76	231,379	8,389	3.6
1976-77	257,835	9,828	3.8
1977-78	289,248	11,388	3.8
1978-79	311,237	12,954	4.2
1979-80	340,488	14,786	4.3

SOURCE: Engineering Manpower Commission; reports from 1969—1979-80.

SOURCE: Reprinted from James E. Blackwell, *Mainstreaming Outsiders: The Production of Black Professionals*. Bayside, New York: General Hall Publishing Co., 1981.

TABLE 15

BACHELOR'S ENGINEERING DEGREES BY RACE AND YEAR, 1970-79—ALL INSTITUTIONS COMBINED

Year	Total B.S. Degrees Awarded	Total B.S. Awarded Black Students	Percent of Total
1969-70	42,966*	378	.8
1970-71	43,167*	407	.9
1971-72	44,190	579	1.3
1972-73	43,429	657	1.5
1973-74	41,407	796	1.8
1974-75	38,210	734	2.0
1975-76	37,970	777	2.0
1976-77	40,095	844	2.1
1977-78	46,091	894	2.1
1978-79	52,598	901	2.0
Totals	**430,123**	**6,967**	**1.6**

*Figures for black students are understated because they do not include data from non-reporting institutions.

SOURCE: The Engineering Manpower Commission.

SOURCE: Reprinted from James E. Blackwell, *Mainstreaming Outsiders: The Production of Black Professionals*. Bayside, New York: General Hall Publishing Co., 1981.

comparison of the data on Tables 15 and 16 shows that there is a monumental problem of retention among black students in Engineering. Almost two-thirds of black freshmen in Engineering dropout of the field before completing degree requirements.

Although the number of blacks graduated with first professional degrees in Engineering is now approaching 1,000 each year, that number is clearly insufficient to meet current demands. For instance, blacks continue to be woefully underrepresented in the graduate schools of this profession. As with the case of white students, graduate schools are finding it all but impossible to compete with the private sector in attracting college graduates. A person with a B.S. in Engineering can often earn a higher salary than that paid by many institutions to their newly minted Ph.D, holding the rank of Assistant Professor. This discrepancy is little incentive to young people to disregard lucrative offers by the major oil companies, the computer industry, and other private firms to enroll in graduate school in quest of an underpaid faculty position. Consequently, there are some 2,500 faculty positions vacant in Engineering Departments around the nation. In addition the faculty problem is further complicated by agreements made between those who wish to pursue graduate education and their employers that that opportunity can be met while employed. With training supported by their firms, such persons are even less likely to be attracted to the teaching profession (Blackwell, 1981).

Degrees Earned: Even though the number of blacks being graduated from college with degrees in Engineering and other disciplines is increasing, they remain underrepresented in the total number of degrees earned. According to National Center for Education Statistics, of the 916,347 bachelor's degrees earned in the United States during the 1978–79 academic year, only 60,130 (or 6.4 percent) were received by blacks. Given the 14 percent of blacks in the college-age population, the underrepresentation of blacks in degree output is both apparent and intolerable.

Graduate and Professional Studies

Invariably, assessments of access of black students to graduate schools and of their graduation rates inescapably conclude that the nation will not reach parity in the production of black doctoral and professional degrees in the near future. (See Table 16.) One explanation for this situation is that the nation is not en-

TABLE 16

DOCTORATES AWARDED U.S. BLACK CITIZENS BY FIELD, PERCENT OF TOTAL DOCTORATES, PERCENT OF TOTAL AWARDED BLACK AMERICANS BY YEARS, 1973-79

Fields	1973	1974	1975	1976	1977	1978	1979
Physical Sciences							
*Total Degrees	4338	4892	4760	4445	4369	4193	4298
Black Citizens	45	46	36	27	41	51	48
% of Degrees/Blk	6.1	5.4	3.6	2.5	3.8	5.0	4.6
Engineering							
Total Degrees	2738	3144	2959	2791	2641	2423	2494
Black Citizens	27	16	11	12	11	9	17
% of Degrees/Blk	1.0	1.9	1.1	1.1	1.1	.9	1.6
Life Sciences							
Total Degrees	4073	4894	5022	4971	4767	4887	5076
Black Citizens	96	69	55	63	55	59	52**—
% of Degrees/Blk	13.1	8.2	5.6	5.8	5.3	6.7	5.0
Social Sciences							
Total Degrees	4796	6156	6307	6583	6504	6543	6379
Black Citizens	87	107	159	172	179	191	206**
% of Degrees/Blk	11.8	12.6	16.1	15.9	17.9	18.6	19.6
Arts & Sciences							
Total Degrees	4461	5174	5046	4883	4559	4235	4143
Black Citizens	74	75	59	91	96	75	119
% of Degrees/Blk	10.1	8.9	8.9	8.4	8.6	9.8	11.3
Education							
Total Degrees	5670	7261	7349	7727	7448	7190	7370
Black Citizens	382	501	605	667	665	583	556
% of Degrees/Blk	52.0	59.2	61.2	61.5	60.0	56.7	53.0
Professions							
Total Degrees	1151	1421	1446	1474	1340	1454	1414(1413)***
Black Citizens	24	32	34	53	41	46	52
% of Degrees/Blk	2.4	3.8	3.5	4.9	3.7	4.5	5.0
Total Degrees							
U.S. Citizens	27,129	26,827	27,009	27,195	26,007	26,529	25,369
Total Degrees-	581	846	989	1,085	1,109	1,029	1,050
Blk & % Blk							
Citizens	(2.1)	(3.1)	(3.6)	(4.0)	(4.2)	(3.8)	(4.1)
All Persons Comb.	32,727	33,000	32,913	32,923	31,672	30,850	31,200

Years: 1973–1979

*Totals include degrees awarded to all students in these fields, irrespective of citizenship
**—These numbers may be slightly inflated due to percentage rounding off
***The number in parenthesis refers to degrees classified this particular year as in the reaching fields
SOURCES: Compiled from data provided by National Academy of Sciences: Commission on Human Resources. Reprinted from James E. Blackwell, *Mainstreaming Outsiders: The Production of Black Professionals.* Bayside, New York: General Hall Publishing Co., 1981.

rolling many black students in its graduate and professional schools despite the increasing absolute numbers of blacks with baccalaureate degrees. It appears that the percentage representation of blacks in graduate schools, for instance, has now plateaued at about 5.6 to 6.0 percent of total graduate enrollment.

In *Mainstreaming Outsiders: The Production of Black Professionals*, the author comments:

> The proportion of black students enrolled in graduate schools increased steadily throughout the decade of the 1970s. In 1972, black graduate students comprised 4.2 percent of all students inrolled in U.S. graduate schools. There was a 1 percent increase, to 5.2 percent, in their proportion by 1973. By 1975, their rate rose to 6.4 percent of total graduate school enrollment. Since 1976, it appears that the percentage of black graduate students has leveled off to about 6.0 percent of total graduate enrollment. According to the latest available data, there are approximately 1,076,980 students enrolled in all of the nation's graduate schools. Of that number, approximately 61,923 are black (Blackwell, 1981, 290).

The 61,923 black graduate students enrolled in 1980 is a noticeable decline from the 65,000 reported by the Institute for Service to Education for 1975. Of that number, 63.4 percent were first-year graduate students (National Advisory Committee, 1979). This decline in the number of graduate students among blacks is not shared by other minority students. For other minority groups, their percentage in graduate schools nationwide is beginning to rise. However, one cannot be excited about the 2.5 percent representation in graduate schools for Asians or particularly sanguine about the 2.6 percent comprised by Hispanic students in graduate schools. All groups are woefully underrepresented in graduate education (Fred M. Hechinger, 1980).

Specific institutions, especially large research-oriented graduate schools, reported a disturbing decrease in the enrollment of black and other minority students in 1980 over their 1979 figures. For example, Stanford University reported a 50 percent decline in the number of its minority students in Fall 1980 (i.e., from 87 to 37 students). The University of Michigan indicated a drop in the number of Black, Hispanic, and Native Indian students from 551 in 1979 to 453 in 1980. The University of California/Berkeley reported a decline from 712 minority students in 1979 to 649 in

1980. The decline at Princeton was from 219 to 165 over the same period and the Harvard Graduate School of Arts and Sciences enrolled only nine new minority students in 1980, compared to 21 in 1979 (Hechinger, 1980).*

According to the Council of Graduate Schools in the United States, applications to the nation's graduate schools in general have declined over the past few years. Such reductions are attributed to such factors as cutbacks on the number of fellowships, scholarships, and grants available to potential graduate students, difficulties in obtaining loans at the same time that tuition rates are being raised, and the employment crisis, which means that many potentially successful graduate students are confronted with "limited job prospects" once the doctorate is obtained. Hence, many of these students opt for other available alternatives (Magarrell, 1980).

In addition to these factors, Blackwell maintains that a negative institutional climate is an impediment of major significance to black students who might otherwise apply and enroll in graduate and professional school programs. This variable of institutional climate includes, inter alia, the reputation attributed to an institution with respect to its treatment of black and other minority students and the presence of black faculty in the institution. His study showed that the most powerful predictor of success in the enrollment of black students at the professional school level was the presence and number of black faculty in the school. In other words, what is suggested here is that those institutions which do a better job of increasing the visibility of black faculty also do a better job of recruiting and enrolling black students (Blackwell, 1981).

Based upon data provided by the National Board of Graduate Education in 1976, the National Advisory Committee on Black Higher Education indicated that most of the black graduate schools with doctoral degree programs were comparatively limited in the programs offered. Whereas Howard University offered doctoral degrees in 20 areas, only four areas were offered at Atlanta University, three at Meharry Medical College, and one at Texas Southern University (National Advisory Committee, September 1979). Program offerings today are limited at black

*These enrollment figures included both Master's and Doctoral students.

graduate schools for several reasons. These include inadequate financial resources required for the development of strong and attractive graduate programs, inability to attract and hold sufficient numbers of black faculty with the specializations and research skills required for the development and maintenance of additional programs, competition with white institutions for students, resources, and faculty.

Despite the difficulties encountered by black graduate schools, their importance for providing access to educational opportunity for black students should by no means be undervalued. For instance, Jean M. Lynch reported in 1979 that the historically black colleges with graduate programs in the South enrolled 90 percent of all black graduate students in Agriculture and Natural Resources, 71 percent of those in the Biological Sciences, 54 percent of those in the Physical Sciences, 99 percent of those in Dentistry, and 58 percent of those in Law (Jean M. Lynch, 1979).

This importance can be further illustrated by data which suggest limited access of black graduate and professional students to non-black institutions in the same state in which black graduate schools are located and in the production rate of black and white institutions. For instance, in 1976, no blacks received a degree in Veterinary Medicine from Auburn University in Alabama but 26 of the 40 DVM degrees awarded by Tuskegee Institute went to black students (National Advisory Committee, January 1979; Blackwell, 1981). Two-thirds of all law degrees awarded to blacks in Texas were conferred by Texas Southern University and 71 percent of all Law degrees received by blacks in North Carolina that year were awarded by North Carolina Central University. In Tennessee, Meharry Medical College conferred 96 percent of all D.D.S. degrees and 92 percent of all M.D. degrees awarded to blacks in that state in 1976 (National Advisory Committee, January 1979). In effect, black institutions did a better job of producing black professionals than did white institutions located in the same state.

Doctoral Degrees: Because of the paucity of black students enrolled in graduate schools and due to a number of reasons cited elsewhere, the production of blacks with doctoral degrees is far below parity. As shown in Table 16, the number of doctoral degrees awarded to blacks between 1973 and 1979 increased dramatically. The 1979 figure of 1,055 was almost double that of the 581 doctoral degrees awarded to blacks in 1973. However, Black Americans still receive only about 5.0 percent of all doctoral degrees conferred each year in the United States (Table 17).

TABLE 17

DOCTORATES AWARDED TO BLACK AMERICANS BY SEX AND YEAR, 1973-79

Year	Total Doctorates Awarded Black Americans	Percent Black of Total	Men	Percent	Women	Percent
1973[a]	581	2.4	—	—	—	—
1974[b]	846	3.8	580	68.6	264	31.4
1975	989	3.3	642	64.9	347	35.1
1976	1,085	4.9	647	59.6	438	40.4
1977	1,109	3.7	681	61.4	428	38.6
1978	1,029	4.5	581	56.5	448	43.5
1979	1,055	5.0	551	52.2	504	47.8
Total	**6,694[a]**	**3.9**	**3,882[b]**	**60.2**	**2,929[b]**	**39.8**

a = No breakdown by sex and race available

b = These figures are for 1974-79 only. They may be inflated by 2 in total after rounding off.

SOURCE: Constructed from Data provided by the National Academy of Sciences, Commission on Human Resources.

SOURCE: Reprinted from James E. Blackwell, *Mainstreaming Outsiders: The Production of Black Professionals*. Bayside, New York: General Hall Publishing Co., 1981.

There is a major problem of maldistribution of the doctoral degrees earned by blacks. This situation poses a critical problem for those institutions conscientiously attempting to increase the number of black faculty on their campuses. It becomes exceedingly difficult to accomplish such goals when over half of the doctoral degrees earned each year (53 percent) are in Education while only 1.6 percent are in Engineering. In 1979, 5.0 percent of doctoral degrees awarded to blacks were in the Life Sciences, 4.6 percent were in Physical Sciences, 11.3 percent were in Arts and Sciences, and 19.6 percent were in the Social Sciences. Five percent of the doctoral degrees were in the professions. In that year, however, only 1,050 blacks received doctoral degrees.

Clearly, it is time to move forward from laudatory pronouncements and agreement about the need to improve the participation of black students in graduate and professional schools. Conscientious efforts, constructive programs, and a renewed commitment of resources are all vital for the achievement of this goal.

Desegregation of Faculty and Administrators

An essential step toward the elimination of all vestiges of inequality of educational opportunity is to equalize faculty and administrators in higher education.

In a 1981 study of hiring, promotion, tenuring and salary practices among the traditionally white institutions (TWIs) in eight of the "Adams States,"* Anne S. Pruitt found that blacks were underrepresented at all faculty, administrative, and executive ranks. Her study revealed both race and sex differences among institutions located in the "Adams States" in the various occupational activities normally observed in colleges and universities. Specifically, blacks, male and female, and women, white or black, were less likely to be hired, promoted, tenured, appointed to managerial, administrative and/or executive positions, or paid high salaries than were white males (Anne S. Pruitt, 1981).

For instance, in 1977, the TWIs in the eight States employed a total of 199,561 persons. The faculty accounted for 36 percent of all workers. Black faculty comprised a mere 1.6 percent of all faculty in the TWIs. Fifty-seven percent of all faculty were on 9-10 month contracts. Of that number, 3.2 percent were black. White males constituted 71 percent of all faculty on 9–10 month contracts; white females, 26 percent; black females, 2 percent; and black males represented a mere percent of all faculty in this category (Pruitt, 1981).

Almost 42 percent (41.7 percent) of the white males received the top salaries offered (Level 5 = $19,000 to $24,999 and Level 6, the highest, = $25,000 and more). This figure compared to 24 percent for black males, 17 percent for white females and eight percent for black females whose salaries were in these ranges (Pruitt, 1981, 22).

Discrepancies were also noted in the distribution of tenure and faculty according to rank, race, and sex. In 1977, "Tenured faculty represented 54.4 percent of all full-time faculty" in the TWIs. Of that group, only 1.8 percent were black. Blacks, male and female, and white women were less likely to hold the rank of Professor. Black and white males were almost equally distributed among the percents of Associate Professor. But, women of

*The eight "Adams States" studies were Arkansas, Florida, Georgia, Maryland, North Carolina, Oklahoma, Pennsylvania, and Virginia.

both races were concentrated at the rank of Assistant Professor among full-time tenured faculty (Table 18). However, white women were considerably more likely to approach white and black males in their proportions located at the Associate Professor rank and black women were far more likely to be concentrated at the Assistant Professor rank.

Pruitt also noted that blacks, in general, were more likely to be in nontenured "on track" faculty positions. But, when she observed a 43.4 percent loss of black faculty at the Associate Professor rank between 1975 and 1977, she concluded that a significant number of blacks were leaving the systems before promotion and tenure. What is also suggested here is that a substantial proportion of the black probationary "on track" faculty *failed* to receive tenure and *failed* to be promoted at the TWIs.

With respect to executive, administrative and managerial positions, her data showed the dominance of white males at the highest positions and maximum salaries. Of the 28,417 persons in this employment category, more than half, 15,371, were white males. Of this number, about 25 percent were paid in excess of $25,000 per year; 23.4 percent were paid from $19,999 to $24,999, but less than ten percent (8.2 percent) were paid salaries in the lowest level of below $9,999. White females represented the next largest number with 10,933 of all executives, managers and administrators. However, only 1.5 percent were paid salaries in excess of $35,000 and 6.0 percent earned in excess of $19,999. White females tended to be concentrated in the salary brackets of $10,000 to $12,999 (42.1 percent) and $13,000 to $15,999 (25.2 percent).

Black females constituted the next largest segment in this occupational category, with 1,177 persons. However, 20 percent of black females were paid less than $10,000; 33.5 percent were paid between $10,000 and $12,999 and 28.4 percent received from $13,000 to $15,999 per year. Only 2.8 percent were in the highest salary level. Black males, on the other hand, represented the smallest number in this group of employees, with 936 persons in 1977. Although 8.4 percent of them received salaries within the highest bracket, they tended to be concentrated in the middle income levels: 26 percent between $13,000 and $15,999; 20.9 percent between $16,000 and $18,999; and 20.5 percent between $10,000 and $12,999; 7.4 percent received salaries below the $10,000 level.

TABLE 18

RANK OF BLACK AND WHITE, FULL-TIME TENURED FACULTY BY SEX FOR *ADAMS* STATES IN 1975 AND 1977

Faculty[a]	Total			Rank: Professor			Rank: Associate Professor			Rank: Assistant Professor			Rank: Other		
	1975	1977	% Δ[b]	1975	1977	% Δ	1975	1977	% Δ	1975	1977	% Δ	1975	1977	% Δ
WM N	21,360	23,176		8,213	9,290		8,392	9,250		2,919	3,113		1,836	1,513	
%			0	38.4	40.0	+1.6	39.2	39.9	+0.7	13.6	13.4	−0.2	8.5	6.5	−2.0
BM N	223	295		46	69		87	118		38	58		52	50	
%			+0.2	20.6	23.3	+2.7	39.0	40.0	+1.0	17.0	19.6	+2.6	23.3	16.9	−6.4
WF N	4,808	5,307		833	1,042		1,648	1,871		1,384	1,514		943	880	
%			+0.2	17.3	19.6	+2.3	34.2	35.2	+1.0	28.7	28.5	−0.2	19.6	16.5	−3.1
BF N	181	256		14	53		30	66		49	70		88	67	
%			+0.2	7.7	20.7	+13.0	16.5	25.7	+9.2	27.0	27.3	+0.3	48.6	26.1	−22.5
Total N	26,572	29,034		9,106	10,454		10,157	11,315		4,390	4,755		2,919	2,510	
%				34.2	36.0	+1.8	38.2	38.9	+0.7	16.5	16.3	−0.2	10.9	8.6	−2.3

[a] Faculty: WM — white male
BM — black male
WF — white female
BF — black female

[b] Change in Percentage between 1975 and 1977.

SOURCE: Reprinted from Anne S. Pruitt, *Black Employees in Traditionally White Institutions in the Adams States, 1975 to 1977*. Atlanta: Southern Education Foundation, 1981.

Hiring practices have not resulted in appreciable improvements in the distribution of blacks in occupational categories in the TWIs. For instance, 85 percent of the "new hires" in 1977 were white. The largest category of new hires among blacks were in secretarial/clerical, technical/paraprofessional, skilled crafts positions. Only 8.7 percent of the new hires within the black population of those newly hired were faculty appointments, compared to 66.6 percent of faculty appointments for whites. Black faculty appointments tend to be non-tenured. This is not indistinct from most appointments for all faculty; however, improvements in the proportion of tenured black faculty can only occur by increases in the number of faculty appointed with tenure when the trend suggests that a significant number of blacks depart from the TWIs *before* being promoted with tenure.

Conclusions

The participation of black students in higher education is not uniform across levels, although national data show an increasing presence of blacks in American colleges and universities. When these data are disaggregated, it is quite apparent that the influx of black students into two-year colleges accounts for a substantial proportion of the yearly increase observed over the past decade. In general, the rate of growth of black student enrollment in the predominantly white colleges and universities fluctuates. Although the South has made more progress in the desegregation of higher education, it remains the most segregated region in the nation with respect to access of black students to the various levels of higher education.

Black student enrollment in the "Adams States" has increased in the traditionally white institutions (TWIs) but blacks remain particularly underrepresented in these institutions. This is especially noticeable with respect to four-year institutions and in states with a well-developed two-year college system. In those states, the trend appears to be higher enrollment of blacks in the two-year colleges and low enrollment of blacks in the TWIs. Whenever increases in black student enrollment in the TWIs occur, there is a profoundly negative impact on the historically black institutions (HBIs). This situation raises serious questions of institutional viability and survival among the state-supported HBIs. It also demands funnelling of financial resources and other necessary support to maintain and enrich the overall quality of the HBIs. It requires an increase in the number and proportion of "other race" students enrolled in the HBIs to assure adequate enrollment as the process of desegregation continues.

In general, black student enrollment in graduate and professional schools has stabilized at a level far below that required to attain parity or, for that matter, to provide a semblance of equal educational opportunity. At the graduate level, blacks represent between 5.6 and 6.0 percent of the more than 61,000 graduate students in the United States. Only about 4 percent of all doctorates conferred in the United States are received by black Americans. At the current rate of production, it is not likely that parity between blacks and whites in the number of doctoral degrees earned will be reached in the next fifty years.

Parity is less likely to be reached in the production of black professionals in such fields as medicine, law, optometry, veterinary medicine, and pharmacy (Blackwell, 1981). Although this paper did not analyze differences between "Adams States" and states not under such litigation, there is empirical evidence to show that even with increasing access to professional schools in those states, the actual enrollment of black students in the public professional schools of those states is low. In many instances, enrollment of black students in the professional schools of the "Adams States" is much lower than it is in several states outside the Adams jurisdiction. In many non-Adams States concrete steps taken to insure greater access across racial lines have had positive results (Blackwell, 1981).

While financial resources and support, such as fellowships, loans, research and teaching assistantships are often critical and wanting with respect to distribution among black students, other factors are also salient with respect to stimulating equality of educational opportunity. One such factor is equity in access, distribution, promotion, and salary of black faculty and administrators (Pruitt, 1981). Faculty members are essential as role models, too. In fact, a high statistical correlation has been demonstrated between the presence of black faculty and the enrollment of black students in professional schools.

The most important conclusion to be drawn from the analysis is the need for increasing the participation, enrollment, and graduation of black students in and from all levels of the higher education system continues to be paramount. The magnitude of this need suggests that a new momentum is required to advance the desegregation process beyond what appears to be a calculated retardation. Meeting that need requires not only commitment to enforce court decisions but other factors indicating the following: (1) improvements in job opportunities, wages, and salaries for black teenagers and adults, (2) aggressive recruitment and enrollment of black students, (3) the creation of more positive institutional climates in colleges and universities that will facilitate both access and retention, and (4) higher visibility of black graduates in the work force. In the mean time, black students must be motivated to learn more, must become self-starters, and maintain the drive to succeed even in the face of adversities.

References

Astin, Alexander W. *Preventing Students From Dropping Out.* San Francisco: Jossey-Bass, 1975.

________. *The Myth of Equal Access in Public Higher Education.* Atlanta: Southern Education Foundation, 1975.

Astin, Helen, and Alexander, et al., *Higher Education and the Disadvantaged Student.* Washington, D.C. Human Science Press, 1972.

Astin, Helen S., and Patricia H. Cross, *Characteristics of Entering Black Freshmen in Predominantly Black and Predominantly White Institutions: A Normative Report,* Los Angeles: Higher Education Research Institute, November 1977.

Barron, Jose (Pepe) "Chicanos in the Community College," *AAJC Journal.* #2 42(9) (1972), 23-26.

"Blacks in America: 25 Years of Radical Change." *U.S. News and World Report.* May 14, 1979, pp. 49-56.

Blackwell, James E. *Mainstreaming Outsiders: The Production of Black Professionals.* New York: General Hall Publishing Co., 1981.

________. "The Access of Black Students to Medical and Law Schools: Trends and Bakke Implications," in Gail Thomas (ed.), *Black Students in Higher Education: Conditions and Experiences in the 1970s.* Westport, Conn: Greenwood Press, 1981.

________. *The Black Community: Diversity and Unity.* New York: Harper and Row, 1975.

Bowles, Samuel and Herbert Gintis. *Schooling in America, Educational Reform and Contradictions of Economic Life.* New York: Basic Books, 1976.

Brazziel, William and Marian, *Recent College and University Enrollment Patterns of Black Students in States Affected by Adams-Califano Litigation.* Atlanta: Southern Education Foundation, 1981.

Gleaser, Edmund J. *Project Focus: A Study of Community Colleges.* New York: McGraw-Hill, 1973.

Grant, W. Vance and Leo J. Eldon, *Digest of Education Statistics 1980.* Washington, D.C.: National Center for Education Statistics, 1980.

Grigg, Charles M., *Access, Retention and Progression of Black Students Through the Two-Tier Florida System of Higher Education.* Atlanta: Southern Education Foundation, 1981.

Hechinger, Fred M. "Affirmative Action Headed for Hard Times," *New York Times.* December 16, 1980, p. C-4.

Holsendoplh, Ernest "Black Presence Grows in Higher Education," *New York Times.* November 14, 1976, p. 15.

Institute for the Study of Educational Policy. *Equal Educational Opportunity for Blacks in U.S. Higher Education, An Assessment.* Washington, D.C. Howard University Press, 1976.

________. *Equal Educational Opportunity. More Promises Than Progress.* Washington, D.C.: Howard University Press, 1976.

________. *Minorities in Two Year Colleges.* Washington, D.C.: Howard University Press, 1980.

Jacobson, Robert L. "Black Graduate Schools Caught in Critical Dilemma, *The Chronicle of Higher Education,* February 22, 1977, p. 1.

Karabel, Jerome. "Community Colleges and Social Stratification," *Harvard Educational Review.* 42: 4 (November 1974), pp. 521-562.

King, Joe. "The Perceptions of Black High School Students Toward Vocational and Technical Education Programs," *The Journal of Negro Education* 66:4 (Fall 1977), pp. 430-442.

Lynch, Jean M. *Maximizing Productivity in Thirty-Two Black Graduate Schools.* Prepared for U.S. Office of Education, DHEW, Contract Number 300770397, 1979, cited in *Black Colleges and Universities: An Essential Component of A Diverse System of Higher Education.*

Magarrell, Jack. "Applications to Graduate Schools Drop: Universities Blame Economic Conditions," *The Chronicle of Higher Education.* May 27, 1980, p. 5.

________., "Big Freshman Class of 2.5 Million Boosts Enrollment to 11.7 Million," *The Chronicle of Higher Education,* May 12, 1980, p. 1.

________. "Fall Enrollment Sets Record Despite Few 18-Year-Olds," *The Chronicle of Higher Education*, November 10, 1980, p. 3.

Middleton, Lorenzo. "Black Agriculture Schools Demand 'Fair Share' of Support," *The Chronicle of Higher Education.* December 3, 1979, p. 5.

Mingle, James R. *Black Enrollment in Higher Education: Trends in the Nation and the South.* Atlanta: Southern Regional Education Board, 1978.

———. "The Opening of White Colleges and Universities to Black Students," in Gail Thomas (ed.), *Black Students in Higher Education.* Westport, Conn: Greenwood Press, 1981.

"Minorities' Share of College Enrollment, Only 8 PCT. in 1969, Was 13 PCT. in 1977," *The Chronicle of Higher Education.* October 16, 1978, p. 18.

Moore, William. *Against the Odds: The Disadvantaged Student in the Community College.* San Francisco: Jossey-Bass, 1970.

Moore, William, and Lonnie Wagstaff. *Black Educators in White Colleges.* San Francisco: Jossey-Bass, 1974.

National Advisory Committee on Black Higher Education and Black Colleges and Universities. *Access of Black Americans to Higher Education: How Open is the Door?* Washington, D.C.: U.S. Government Printing Office, January 1979.

———. *Black Colleges and Universities: An Essential Component of a Diverse System of Higher Education.* Washington, D.C.: U.S. Government Printing Office, September 1979.

National Advisory Committee. *Higher Education Equity: The Crisis of Appearance Versus Reality*: Washington, D.C. U.S. Government Printing Office, 1978.

———. *Target Date. 2000 AD: Higher Education and Equity for Black Americans. Volume 1.* Washington, D.C.: U.S. Government Printing Office, September 1980.

National Board on Graduate Education. *Minority Group Participation in Graduate Education.* Washington, D.C.: National Academy of Sciences, June 1976.

Ogbu, John U. *Minority Student Education and Caste, The American System in Cross-Cultural Perspectives.* New York: Academic Press, 1978.

Olivas, Michael. *The Dilemma of Access: Minorities in Two-Year Colleges.* Washington, D.C.: Howard University Press, 1979.

"Proportions of Americans Who Have Attended College Rose During the 1970s, Census Bureau Reports," *The Chronicle of Higher Education*, October 20, 1980, p. 2.

Pruitt, Anne S. *Black Employees in Traditional White Institutions in the Adams States: 1975 to 1977.* Atlanta: The Southern Education Foundation, 1981.

"Rate of Enrollment Growth Among Blacks is Slowing: Surpassed by Hispanics," *The Chronicle of Higher Education.* August 25, 1980, p. 9.

Thomas, Gail (ed.), *Black Students in Higher Education: Conditions and Experiences in the 1970s.* Westport, Conn: Greenwood Press, 1981.

"Undergraduate Enrollment, by Race, in U.S. Colleges and Universities." *The Chronicle of Higher Education.* February 2, 1981, pp. 6-14.

U.S. Bureau of the Census. *The Social and Economic Status of the Black Population in the United States: An Historical View, 1790–1978* (Current Population Reports, Special Series P-23, No. 80). Washington, D.C.: U.S. Government Printing Office, 1978.

United States Commission on Civil Rights. *The Black/White Colleges: Dismantling the Dual System of Higher Education.* Washington, D.C.: U.S. Government Printing Office, Clearinghouse Publication 66, April 1981.

Wright, Stephen J. *The Black Educational Policy Researcher: An Untapped National Resource.* Washington, D.C.: National Advisory Committee.

"Years of School Completed by Americans." *The Chronicle of Higher Education*, September 13, 1976, p. 12.

3 A Political Taxonomy of Desegregation

Jewel L. Prestage

The education of black Americans has never been a priority item on the American public agenda. An examination of the accepted state desegregation *Plans* would seem to support the contention that this pattern is likely to continue into the foreseeable future. Despite variations in their responses to the criteria that are to guide development of *Plans*, the states, in the main, emerge committed to perpetuation of those long-term policies and practices which have forced blacks into a continuous quest for educational equity at all levels in the system.

Historical Background

Black public higher education began during the Reconstruction period, the first opportunity which blacks had to participate in the traditional political process in significant numbers. By 1876 some eight public institutions of higher education for Blacks had been established. According to one historian, black colleges and universities owe their origin to political deals made by black men who believed in the power of education and white men who believed in the inability of blacks to profit from education. This conflict, he asserts, has prevailed over time.

Segregation has been endemic to public higher education for Blacks from the inception. Constitutional credence was given to segregation as a practice in *Plessy* v. *Ferguson* in 1896. Although the case involved transportation, the principle of "separate but equal" enunciated by the Supreme Court therein was applied to education and other dimensions of life and culture. Congress had given impetus to the practice of racial segregation in the 1890 Morrill Act establishing separate land grant colleges for blacks. In a series of cases the United States Supreme Court upheld "separate but equal." What resulted were two systems of higher education "separate but *unequal,*" one black and one white. Failure to fully implement the *Plessy* rule in public higher education for blacks was the subject of a series of court cases. Out-of-state tuition in lieu of state based graduate and professional education, intra-university segregation of blacks admitted to previously all white graduate schools, and the inequality of tangible and intangible elements in separate black and white law schools were among practices challenged. The Supreme Court declared the out-of-state tuition practice a violation of the 14th Amendment, and also found segregation by race inside a university to be unlawful in the *Gaines* and *McLaurin* Cases, respectively. Separate law schools for blacks and whites in Texas were found to be unequal in terms of both tangible and intangible factors in *Sweat* v. *Painter*. However, it was in the case of *Brown* v. *Board of Education of Topeka*, affecting elementary and secondary education, that the U.S. Supreme Court dealt the death blow to "separate but equal in education." The case was decided on May 17, 1954, under provisions of the 14th Amendment.

The legal bases for the challenge to segregated higher education are the 14th Amendment and Title VI of the Civil Rights Act of 1964. Title VI states:

> No person in the United States shall, on the ground of race, color or national origin be excluded from participation in or be denied the benefits of, or be subjected to discrimination under any program or activity receiving Federal financial assistance.

The Adams Cases

The first attempt to utilize principles established in the Brown Case in higher education occurred when the NAACP Legal Defense Fund brought suit in the U.S. District Court in Washington, D.C., in the Fall of 1970, charging the U.S. Department of Health, Education and Welfare with continuing to provide funds to operate public educational institutions in the states practicing racial discrimination. The case, *Adams* v. *Richardson*, which involved John Quincy Adams, a black man from Mississippi and his 6 children, and Elliott Richardson, then Secretary of Health, Education and Welfare, was a comprehensive class action suit against the federal government seeking to cut off federal funds to the affected states. Legal basis for the suit was Title VI of the 1964 Civil Rights Act cited above.

In 1969 and 1970 HEW had notified 10 states (Arkansas, Florida, Georgia, Louisiana, Maryland, Mississippi, North Carolina, Oklahoma, Pennsylvania, Virginia) that they must devise plans for desegregation of their postsecondary institutions but had failed to follow up on the matter, resulting in continued funding of racially identifiable institutions of higher education. The decision was rendered by the district court and upheld by the U.S. Court of Appeals in June 1973. The Courts held that HEW had failed to enforce compliance with Title VI. The ten states were ordered to submit plans for the desegregation of their systems of higher education and HEW was given until June 1974 to either accept the plans or to initiate court action to cut off federal funds. By June 1974, HEW had accepted plans from 8 of the 10 states. Louisiana refused to submit a plan, while Mississippi's Plan was deemed unacceptable and referred to the Justice Department for legal action.

During the Summer of 1975 HEW sent evaluation letters to states (based on data collected from the eight systems over the previous year) detailing the extent to which commitments made in the Plans were not kept. HEW indicated that if affirmative responses did not come, enforcement action would be taken immediately. Georgia was exempted because its plan was found to be in substantial compliance. In August 1975, the Legal Defense Fund charged that HEW had not fulfilled requirements of the 1973 decision. Hearings on the Legal Defense Fund charge were scheduled by the district court for January 1977. In the interim (December 1975) HEW notified Maryland that it would initiate enforcement proceedings against the state for failure to adequately implement its statewide desegregation plan. Maryland responded by seeking and obtaining an injunction restraining HEW from commencing enforcement proceedings designed to cut off federal funds.

An annexed *amicus curiae* brief was filed with the court by the National Association for Equal Opportunity in Higher Education (NAFEO) in March 1976, opposing the Legal Defense Fund's contention that compliance required merger/assimilation of Black institutions into white ones and expressing concern over the extent to which black institutions would be adversely affected. Also relevant was intervention of the state of Pennsylvania as a party defendant in the case. Entry was based on the state's feelings that HEW was not conducting the defense in

Pennsylvania's best interest and that the state might not be able to fulfill requirements for desegregation that might be ruled for the other affected states.

In January 1977 the district court ruled that in the case of six states HEW failed to seek effective desegregation plans and that HEW must prepare new guidelines for states to use in developing desegregation plans for higher education. Of the other four states, Louisiana, Mississippi and Maryland were in litigation and Pennsylvania chose an out of court settlement. Basic ingredients of the new guidelines, according to the decision, were specific objectives, timetables and procedures for implementation.

In January 1977 the new Secretary of HEW, Joseph Califano took office and was given a 90-day period to review *Adams* litigation. On April 1, 1977 a supplemental order and decision was issued by the district court (Adams vs. Califano). The court directed that HEW notify the six states (Arkansas, Florida, Georgia, North Carolina, Oklahoma and Virginia) that their Plans were not in compliance with Title VI and that HEW, within 90 days, transmit to the states the plaintiffs and the court final guidelines for desegregation plans. Each state was to submit a revised plan 60 days after getting guidelines and then HEW was to notify states, within 120 days, as to whether the revised plans were acceptable. During this process the plaintiffs are to have access to "all submitted desegregation plans" and biannual reports.

Review of Selected Plans

Six state plans have been selected for review—Louisiana, North Carolina, South Carolina, Georgia, Florida and Arkansas. Acceptance of these plans were in 1981, except for Arkansas (1978) and Georgia (1979). Documents used for reviews are cited in text.

The specific criteria for developing plans were set forth by HEW and the courts. Five of the criteria serve as the basis for the review of each of the selected plans.

I. Disestablishment of the structure of the dual system
II. Desegregation of student enrollment
III. Desegregation of faculty, administration, staff and governance
IV. Enhancement of historically black institutions
V. Monitoring/Reporting provisions

Louisiana

Louisiana's population was 4,203,972 in 1980 with 1,237,263 black persons. The public institutions of higher education in the state are identified in the plan as follows:

A. Predominantly black institutions
   1. Grambling State University
   2. Southern University—Baton Rouge
   3. Southern University—New Orleans
   4. Southern University—Shreveport-Bossier

B. Predominantly "white institutions"
   1. Louisiana Tech University
   2. University of Southwestern Louisiana
   3. McNeese State University
   4. Nicholls State University
   5. Northeast Louisiana University
   6. Southeastern Louisiana University
   7. Northwestern State University
   8. Louisiana State University—Baton Rouge
   9. University of New Orleans
   10. Louisiana State University—Shreveport
   11. Louisiana State University—Alexandria
   12. Louisiana State University—Eunice
   13. Paul M. Hebert Law Center (LSU-BR)
   14. Louisiana State University Medical Center (Shreveport & New Orleans)
   15. Delgado Junior College
   16. St. Bernard Community College
   17. Bossier Parish Community College

C. Predominantly black professional school
   1. Southern University Law School in Baton Rouge

D. Predominantly white professional schools
   1. Louisiana State Medical Center
   2. Paul M. Hebert Law Center
   3. Louisiana State University School of Veterinary Medicine

Louisiana was one of the ten states originally examined by HEW, but Louisiana refused to submit a Plan, contending that it did not operate a dual system of higher education. The Department of Justice filed a law suit in 1974 and Louisiana submitted a Plan in 1980. That Plan was rejected and the case was to be tried in 1981. A Consent Decree was finalized on September 8, 1981, bringing an end to litigation.

I. *Disestablishment of the Structure of the Dual System.* As a result of programmatic changes at the predominantly black institutions, the role, scope, and mission statement of each institution (as stated in the Master Plan of 1978) shall be revised and the revised statement shall appear in the next update of the Master Plan. Formulation of the Bevised statements will entail participation of management boards and institutions within the state's system of higher education.

New Programs are provided for predominantly black institutions.

SUBR	SUNO	Grambling State
Bachelors—School of Nursing, Rehabilitation Psychology, Environmental Chemistry, and joint baccalaureate degree programs in several allied health fields with LSU Medical Center.	Bachelors—Substance Abuse, Print Journalism, Urban Studies, Criminal Justice, Technology, Transportation, joint baccalaureate degree programs in several allied health fields with LSU Medical Center.	Bachelors—School of Nursing, Joint baccalaureate degree programs in several allied health fields with LSU Medical Center.
Masters—Rehabilitation Psychology, Special Education, Computer Science, M.P.A. from a new School of Public Policy and Urban Affairs (in cooperation with LSU-BR but with degree awarded	Masters—MSW from new School of Social Work	Masters—M.P.A. in Public Administration; M.A.T. in Social Science, Natural Science and Humanities; M.S.W. in Social Welfare; Criminal Justice; Developmental Education; Science Education; M.B.A. in

by Southern University)		cooperation with LA. Tech. with degree awarded by Grambling.
Doctoral—(D.P.A.) Professional Accountancy; (Ed.D. & Ph.D.) Special Education	Doctoral—None	Doctoral—Developmental Education
Other—Six year professional degree in Professional Accountancy; Center for Small Farm Research	Other—A.S. in Computer Science; in the several allied fields where B.S. is offered (health)	Other—A.S. in several allied health fields

Future Program Considerations:

SUBR	SUNO	Grambling State
B.S. Radiological Technology; Early Childhood Education	Bachelors—Nursing	B.S. gerontology
Masters—Agribusiness; Labor Management; Adaptive Physical Education; M.B.A. (Labor-Management Relations)	Masters—Substance Abuse, Criminal Justice	Masters—Science Education
Doctoral—None	Doctoral—None	Doctoral—Science Education; Elementary Education
Other—None	Other—None	Other—School of Law (J.D.); A.S. in Paralegal Studies

If need is documented for an additional state supported School of Pharmacy, it will be located at Southern University—Baton Rouge or Southern University—New Orleans while any new law school will be established at Grambling State University. Further, the Board of Regents will give special consideration to placing new high-demand, high-cost programs at predominantly black institutions. Prior to approval of any new program at any predominantly white institution, the Board of Regents shall assess the impact of such implementation on predominantly black institutions and will not duplicate at a white institution any program approved for a proximate predominantly black institution. In decisions to eliminate a program after review the Board of Regents is committed to act consistent with the objective of enhancing predominantly black institutions. Should the Regents decide to eliminate degree programs pursuant to any academic program review it shall do so in a manner that does not disproportionately affect any predominantly black institution.

II. *Increased Student Enrollment*. The State adopted as goals making the proportion of black high school graduates entering public institutions of higher education equal to the proportion of white high school graduates who do and making the proportion of qualified black Louisiana residents who graduate from undergraduate institutions and enter State graduate and professional schools equal to the proportion of white state residents graduating and entering.

Other-race student interim enrollment goals are set for predominantly white institutions but interim goals for predominantly black institutions are delayed for two years to enable enhancement to be initiated. The open admissions policy for public institutions will be continued for six years and a rather comprehensive program is provided for "other-race" recruitment. Other-race scholarships will be offered in medicine, dentistry, veterinary medicine. Developmental education programs are stipulated for all public institutions in the state. Faculty and student exchange goals for proximate institutions are set forth.

The Nursing Programs at Southern University—Baton Rouge and at Southeastern Louisiana State University should each have 25 percent other-race enrollment.

III. *Desegregation of Faculty, Administration, Staff, Governance*. Louisiana adopts as a goal the increasing of other-race representation on the following boards so that the composition of the membership of each approximately reflects the racial composition of the State's population: Louisiana Board of Regents; Board of Trustees for State Colleges and Universities; Board of Supervisors for Louisiana State University and A and M College.

Further, the State adopts as an interim six-year goal the increasing of other-race representation on the Board of Supervisors of Southern University and A and M College so that its racial composition reflects the racial composition of the State's population inversely. Affirmative steps will be taken to achieve these goals as early as practicable but within a period not to exceed six years. Another goal is that the proportion of black administrators, faculty and staff at each predominantly white public institution be equal to the proportion of black individuals with the required credentials in the relevant labor market area. Each predominantly black institution shall increase its proportion of white administrators, faculty and staff. Goals shall be revised on an annual basis taking into account changes which may occur regarding the availability of qualified blacks for employment at State institutions and at the higher education boards. Each institution is obliged to develop an affirmative action plan. The Board of Regents will develop a Clearinghouse to identify qualified Blacks and facilitate their recruitment to fill vacancies at State institutions. To increase the pool of "other-race" faculty qualified to teach at State institutions a Graduate Fellowship Program is to be established to support persons desiring to complete terminal degrees and committed to teach at other-race institutions.

IV. *Enhancement of Black Institutions.* Faculty development at predominantly Black institutions will be supported by the provision of paid leaves of absence for non-terminal degree holders wishing to complete degree requirements. Faculty exchange programs and cooperative and joint programs are established for proximate institutions. Academic programs at predominantly black institutions will be strengthened and enhanced with specific new programs as stipulated earlier. In terms of capital improvements, the state set as a goal the improvement of existing facilities and the construction of new facilities at predominantly black institutions such that physical plants will be comparable to those available at comparable white institutions. A study to determine capital improvements needs will be developed, under a grant of $148,000 from the Board of Regents and overseen by one expert chosen by the Board of Regents and one chosen by the United States of America. Recommendations from the study are to be reflected in the adjustments in the Board of Regents five-year capital outlay plan by January 1, 1983. Increased financial support will entail funding adequate for the implementation of the Consent Decree, parity funding for Southern University Law School and LSU Law Center per FTE, $285,000 per year for enhancement of Southern University Law School, $200,000 for enhancing management and $1,000,000 per year for general management of Southern and Grambling.

V. *Monitoring and Reporting*. A nine-member Consent Decree Monitoring Committee is established with two members appointed by each of the four boards and the chairman appointed by the Governor. One full-time staff member is assigned and annual reports (statistical and narrative) will be filed.

North Carolina

In 1980 North Carolina's population was 5,874,429 with 1,316,050 Blacks.

All 16 public institutions of higher learning are party of the University of North Carolina. Five are predominantly black: Elizabeth City State University; Fayetteville State University; North Carolina A & T University; North Carolina Central University and Winston-Salem State University.

The eleven white universities are: Appalachian State; East Carolina State; North Carolina State at Raleigh; Pembroke State; University of North Carolina at Asheville; University of North Carolina at Chapel Hill; University of North Carolina at Charlotte; University of North Carolina at Greensboro; University of North Carolina at Wilmington; and West Carolina University. Also there is North Carolina School of the Arts.

The two major research units are those at Chapel Hill and Raleigh; other doctoral university is University of North Carolina at Greensboro. The six comprehensive universities are Appalachian, East Carolina, North Carolina A & T, North Carolina Central, University of North Carolina at Charlotte and West Carolina while the six general baccalaureate campuses are Elizabeth City, Fayetteville, Pembroke, University of North Carolina at Asheville, University of North Carolina at Wilmington and Winston-Salem State.

All institutions are under a single Board of Governors, of whom four were black in 1980.

Along with six Adams states North Carolina submitted a desegregation plan in September, 1977, but the plans of North Carolina, Georgia, and Virginia were rejected by HEW. Negotiations produced acceptable plans for all of the states except North Carolina by March, 1979. Under provisions of Title VI and the *Adams* court decision, enforcement procedures were begun against North Carolina. The state filed suit in U.S. District Court to enjoin any deferral or termination of Federal funds by HEW administrative proceedings and the implementation of HEW desegregation criteria. The district court denied North Carolina's request to halt administrative proceedings but ruled that HEW could neither defer nor terminate federal funds to the University of North Carolina until an administrative hearing had yielded a finding of noncompliance. For North Carolina the Consent Decree of July 13, 1981, ends the series of action which commenced in 1969–70 when HEW started to direct its efforts to the examination of ten states which operated dual systems of public higher education.

I. *Disestablishment of the Dual system.* There were only two changes in missions of institutions in North Carolina. Fayetteville State University was changed from a general baccalaureate university to a comprehensive university and a Graduate Center was established at Winston-Salem State University.

A total of thirty new programs were added at predominantly Black campuses, none at the doctoral level. It was further provided that no fewer than one third of any new degree programs not already in Long Range Planning 1980–85 for comprehensive universities shall be at predominantly black institutions and no fewer than one half in the case of general baccalaureate institutions.

II. *Desegregating Student Enrollments.* North Carolina commits to engage in extensive informational and student recruitment activities to inform black citizens of opportunities within the University of North Carolina and of the prohibition of race/discrimination and the encouragement of racial diversity in constituent institutions, to inform increased numbers of prospective applicants of opportunities in other race institutions, and to promote minority presence at constituent institutions. Some examples of undergraduate recruitment activities are: (1) the division

ACADEMIC PROGRAMS

Elizabeth City	Fayetteville	North Carolina A & T	N. C. Central	Winston-Salem
Remains General baccalaureate	Changed from General baccalaureate to Comprehensive	Remains a Comprehensive University	Remains a Comprehensive University	Remains a General Baccalaureate university
New Programs Computer Science Applied Math Accounting Music	**New Programs** Bachelors: Accounting Art Criminal Justice	**New Programs** Bachelors: Special Education Reading Chemical Engineering Civil Engineering Occupational Safety	**New Programs** Bachelors: Computer Science	**New Programs** Bachelors: Accounting Recreation Theory Economics Communications Spanish Chemistry
Other Graduate Center to continue	**Graduate** Masters Special Education Ed. Administration Business Administration	**Graduate-Masters** Mech. Engineering Agricultural Engineering Applied Math Transportation	**Graduate** Masters Criminal Justice Political Science	**Other** Graduate Center to be established
		Other Media (6-year Advanced Certificate)	**Other** Improvements School of Business Law School	

of the state into eight districts with a predominantly black institution in each; (2) each institution is to make a good faith effort to hire one or more other race admissions officers and use minority presence representation in high school visitations; (3) special contacts for minority student applicants. Examples at the graduate and professional levels are (1) the three major research universities (Chapel Hill, Raleigh, Greensboro) are committed to visit predominantly black institutions (public and private) and (2) all institutions with graduate offerings for in-service teachers must inform all nearby public schools of nondiscriminatory policies; and (3) special financial aid programs for minority presence are established at all levels. Goals for the state are: 15 percent minority presence at black institutions; 10.6 percent minority presence at white institutions.

III. *Desegregation of Faculty, Staff, Administration, Governance.* Affirmative action plans at each constituent institution will be revised by June 30, 1983 and cover the period through December 31, 1986. Plans will reflect anticipated vacancies and anticipated total employees through that date. The two separate categories of employees to be involved are faculty with tenure and tenure track positions and employees in executive, administrative, and managerial positions. Goals shall reflect anticipated vacancies and anticipated total employees and availability of blacks with appropriate degree qualifications.

IV. *Enhancement of Black Institutions.* The state is committed to parity in weighted average financial support for black and white institutions, in student-faculty ratio, in average teaching salary in state funds for budgeted positions, in support for libraries, in summer session instruction, in student financial aid, and in tuition charges. Further, the Faculty Doctoral Study Program of $400,000 annually will continue with priority to Black institutions; doctorate degrees will be required for all new full-time faculty at black institutions and for the conferring of tenure on any faculty unless there are exceptional circumstances. Special conferences of administrative officials in the Black institutions are to be called by University General Administration. With reference to capital improvements, when the state program is completed the buildings constructed before 1979–80 on predominantly black college campuses will be comparable to white campuses; projects for black institutions will receive a type of priority.

V. *Monitoring & Reporting.* The president of the university is responsible for monitoring. Each constituent unit shall submit a detailed report and the chancellors of constituent units shall meet at the University General Administration at least once a year with the president to review these reports.

Reports will be filed by the university each December with counsel for the Government and the Assistant Secretary for Civil Rights of the Department of Education. Items addressed in the report will be (1) actions taken to comply with commitments of Section VI of the Decree (increased minority presence in enrollment and employment); (2) minority presence enrollments at predominantly white and predominantly black institutions; (3) current operations and capital improvement budgets for each comprehensive and baccalaureate institution; (4) implementation of the institutional development plans of each predominantly Black institution.

South Carolina

In 1980 South Carolina's total population was 3,119,208. Of these 948,146 were black.

South Carolina has a total of sixty-three degree-granting postsecondary educational institutions. These include thirty private two- and four-year institutions. The thirty-three public colleges and universities consist of three general types of institutions:

1. *Universities,* providing degree programs through doctorate, emphasizing graduate and professional programs specific to each. There are three universities: Clemson University, the Medical University of South Carolina, and the University of South Carolina at Columbia.
2. *Senior colleges,* emphasizing undergraduate instruction but also offering master's level programs as are appropriate in specific instances. There are nine public senior colleges. Five offer degrees through the master's. One of these is a traditionally black institution, South Carolina State College (SCSC).
3. *Two-Year Colleges,* offering programs through the associate degree level tailored to the specific needs of local communities. There are twenty-two two-year colleges, consisting of five two-year campuses of the University of South Carolina and sixteen technical colleges governed by the State Board for Technical and Comprehensive

Education. One of the sixteen Technical Colleges, Denmark, is predominantly black.

Public postsecondary education institutions in South Carolina are governed by eight separate governing boards: single institutions boards for Clemson University, the University of South Carolina, the Medical University of South Carolina, South Carolina State College, The Citadel, and Winthrop College; the State College Board for the College of Charleston, Frances Marion College, and Lander College; and the State Board for Technical and Comprehensive Education that governs the sixteen technical colleges.

The composition and size of each board is determined by the General Assembly. The total membership includes seventy-two elected by the General Assembly in Joint Session, nineteen state officials serving *ex-officio*, eight appointed by the Governor, seven self-perpetuating, and five selected by the alumni of the institutions.

All public postsecondary educational institutions were established through legislation enacted by the General Assembly, which also provided for the governance of each. The General Assembly determines the majority membership on six of the eight governing boards. Clemson's Board of Trustees included seven self-perpetuating members and six elected by the General Assembly, and, the Governor appoints the majority of the members of the State Board for Technical and Comprehensive Education with the consent of the General Assembly.

The Commission on Higher Education was established by the General Assembly in 1967 as the State coordinating agency in higher education. It is a coordinating body which has authority to approve and recommend termination of programs subject to review by the General Assembly, but otherwise the Commission must rely on persuasion to gain cooperation and support. The Commission includes eighteen members (three from each congressional District) appointed by the Governor with the consent of the majority of the members of the General Assembly from the district.

HEW began a statewide review of the higher education system in South Carolina during the Spring of 1979 with the intent of determining the extent to which the state was in compliance with the Title VI. However, in December of 1980, the U.S. Department of Education had not issued the findings of the reviews to the state and plaintiffs in the Adams litigation took the matter to Court. The Court ordered that the findings be issued within 30 days. On January 7, 1981, Governor Richard W. Riley received a letter stating that the state was not in compliance with Title VI of the Civil Rights Act of 1964 because all vestiges of its former *de jure* racially dual system of public higher education had not been eliminated. A statewide desegregation plan within 60 days of receipt of the letter was requested. Governor Riley requested that the South Carolina Commission on Higher Education assume the responsibility for developing a response. The Commission on Higher Education accepted this responsibility and appointed a Steering Committee and a Technical Committee to aid in the formulation of the response. The Steering Committee consisted of representatives of the Colleges and universities, the general public, the business community, the General Assembly, the Budget and Control Board, the Attorney General's Office, The Governor's Office, and the Commission on Higher Education. The Technical Committee consisted of Commission members and staff, college and university representatives, and research personnel from the offices of public officials and State agency heads serving on the Steering Committee. The response was submitted to the Commission on Higher Education and it approved the response on March 5, 1981, and submitted it to the Governor Richard W. Riley for his approval and transmittal to the U.S. Department of Education.

The South Carolina plan consists of two documents, the *South Carolina Plan for Equity and Equal Opportunity in Public Colleges and Universities* and a supplementary document entitled *South Carolina's Response to OCR's Comments on the South Carolina Plan for Equity and Equal Opportunity in the Public Colleges and Universities.* The plan was approved by the OCR during July, 1981. The first is 245 pages and the second consists of more than 115 pages.

I. *Disestablishment of the Structure of the Dual System.* The mission for each of the thirty-three public institutions in the state system is defined on a basis other than race. The plan denies that black and white institutions (University of South Carolina, Clemson, and South Carolina State College) have similar missions.

The programs provided are as follows:

South Carolina State	*Denmark Technical College*
1. School of Business Administration with 5 new programs	1. Construction Management Technology (2 years)
2. Doctor of Education (Ed.D.)	2. A. S. in Public Service
3. Specialist in Education (Ed.S.)	3. A. S. in Business
4. Agribusiness (B.S.)	
5. Agribusiness (M.S.)	

Existing programs targeted for strengthening are:

South Carolina State	*Denmark Technical College*
History & Political Science	1. Nuclear Science
Math	2. Air Conditioning/ Refrigeration
Communications	3. Welding
Natural Science	4. Machine Tool Technology
Engineering Technology (for accreditation)	
Habilitative Sciences	
Behavioral Sciences	
Industrial Education	

In connection with new programs the state estimates that it will expend $7,800,000 over five years at South Carolina State College, excluding capital improvements. At Denmark Technical College the cost will exceed $550,000 in the first time costs and over $1.1 million for the life of the plan. Overall it is estimated that over $19 million will be expended.

Duplication of program will be reduced by the following actions:

1. University of South Carolina will phase out its Ed.D. program in Educational Administration in favor of this program being offered at South Carolina State College.
2. Clemson will not offer the B.A. and M.S. in Agribusiness if they are offered at South Carolina State College.

II. *Desegregation of Student Enrollment.* South Carolina commits itself to the following goals: increasing proportion of black high school graduates who enter two-year and four-year undergraduate public institutions to equal the proportion of whites who do; to enrolling black graduates of undergraduate institutions in graduate or professional schools in proportion to white entering; to increasing white student enrollment at South Carolina State and Denmark Tech; to increasing the proportion of black students attending and completing traditionally white two-year and four-year public institutions; to extending mobility between 2-year and 4-year colleges; to seeking special support for other-race recruitment and retention programs; to increasing the pool of black potential college students.

III. *Desegregation of Faculty, Administration, Staff, Governance.* A broad commitment is made to increase the number of Black persons appointed to governing boards of public higher education institutions of the state with the promise to submit appropriate proposals to the South Carolina legislature. For those positions not requiring the doctorate, 11.9 percent will be used as the utilization level for blacks in predominantly white colleges and the number of blacks receiving master's degrees from the state's institutions annually will serve as the base for determining the utilization levels in the future. Findings from a national study of blacks in relevant labor market areas with required credentials will be used for positions requiring the doctorate. Commitments are also made to increase blacks on staffs of boards of governance and at all levels of employment.

IV. *Enhancement of Predominantly Black Institutions.* Faculty salaries at South Carolina State will be upgraded to the average salaries of peer institutions through a one time adjustment amount of $349,604. Specific new academic programs are identified above.

The Plan commits the State to capital improvements of $6,300,000 at South Carolina State.

V. *Monitoring & Reporting.* The Commission on Higher Education is charged with responsibility for monitoring the implementation of the Plan. This body is 22 percent black and is the state agency which coordinates the system of public higher education. Each institution will have a campus coordinator whose responsibility is to coordinate the institutional involvement in the planning process. A comprehensive narrative assessment of implementation efforts is due to the Governor and the U.S. Department of Education by August 15.

Georgia

Georgia, with a total population of 5,464,265 and a black population of 1,465,457, was one of the ten states selected by

HEW for compliance review to determine if the state was in violation of Title VI. HEW found Georgia in violation and notified Georgia, requesting a plan on February 26, 1970. Georgia sent a letter to HEW on May 15, 1970 citing progress made in desegregating its institutions of higher education. HEW accepted this letter, though it was not a plan, as adequate action by the state. Later Georgia was asked to provide data describing actions it had taken since February 1970 to eliminate vestiges of the dual system. The state provided a response and on May 19, 1973, HEW notified Georgia that its dual system had not been disestablished, in spite of progress made in increasing black enrollment in some predominantly white universities. New guidelines were developed by HEW in the Summer of 1973 and a deadline of June 1, 1974 was set for states to submit plans. Georgia's plan was formally submitted on June 1, 1974 and approved by HEW on July 19, 1974. Semi-annual reports were submitted from January 1, 1975 to January 1977. The NAACP-Legal Defense Fund, after reviewing progress reports, went back to Court. In April 1977 the Court informed HEW that new guidelines were needed. In July 1977 HEW informed Georgia of the inadequacy of the 1974 plan and directed the state to the new guidelines. Among the major new criteria were:

1. Use of statewide, comprehensive, coordinated plans;
2. Use of specific funding commitments and project goals;
3. Avoidance of any reduction in opportunities for blacks and in status of black colleges;
4. Elimination of unnecessary duplicative programs;
5. Priority to black institutions in placement of new programs; and
6. Increased black utilization of higher education.

Georgia developed a new plan, the fifth segment of which was submitted to HEW on December 13, 1978. The first had been submitted on September 1, 1977; the second on December 15, 1977; the third on March 8, 1978 and the fourth on October 19, 1978. Approval of the plan was given in February 1979. Aspects of the plan were upheld in *Marsha Artis et al.* vs. *Board of Regents of the University System of Georgia et al.* in 1981.

University System of Georgia is made up of:

four Graduate Institutions—providing work through the doctorate and other advanced degrees

1. Georgia Institute of Technology

2. Georgia State University
3. Medical College of Georgia
4. University of Georgia

twelve Senior Colleges—offering undergraduate education and graduate degrees below the doctorate level

Albany State College*	Georgia Southern College
Armstrong State College	Georgia Southwestern College
Augusta College	North Georgia College
Columbus College	Savannah State College*
Fort Valley State College*	Valdosta State College
Georgia College	West Georgia College

*Predominantly black institutions.

Note: Earlier work on Georgia by Professor Robert Holmes is acknowledged.

16 Junior Colleges—offering 2 year transfer programs, associated degrees and 1 and 2 year certificates

Abraham Baldwin Junior College	Floyd Junior College
Albany Junior College	Gainesville Junior College
Atlanta Junior College	Gordon Junior College
Bainbridge Junior College	Kennesaw Junior College
Brunswick Junior College	Macon Junior College
Clayton Junior College	Middle Georgia Junior College
Dalton Junior College	South Georgia Junior College
Emannuel Junior College	Waycross Junior College

The governing body is "The Board of Regents of the University System of Georgia."

I. *Disestablishment of the Dual System.* The mission of each institution is determined without reference to race. Specific roles and missions statements are not detailed in the plan but the three predominantly black institutions are identified as senior colleges and are to remain senior colleges. Duplication of programs is to be eliminated and avoided in future developments. One example of correction involves Savannah State and Armstrong State, located in close proximity. All education programs are transferred to Armstrong and all Business Administration to Savannah State.

New programs in the plan are:

Albany State	*Fort Valley*	*Savannah State*
Criminal Justice Institute	A Rural Life Center with:	B.S. in Environmental

offering B.A.	A.S.—Agr. Econ.	Studies
and M.A.	& Farm	B.S. Chem. Eng.
	Management	Technology
Bachelor's (3)	A.S.—Agr.	B.S.—
Computer	Mechanization	Aeronautical
Science	Technology	Eng.
Social Welfare	B.S.—Agr. Econ.	Technology
Political	& Farm	B.S. in Biology
Science	Management	with Certificate
	B.S. in	in Marine
Master's	Ornamental	Biology
Teacher	Horticulture	A.S.—Marine
Education	B.S.—Agri.	Technology
Business	Mechanizat.	A.S. Computer
Admin.	Technology	Tech.
	M.Ed.—Agr.	
5 programs with	Exten. Ed.	Sole program in
Albany Junior	B.S.—Computer	region in
College	Science	Business
	B.S. Historical	Administration
	Admin.	

II. *Increased Student Enrollment.* A target of 16 percent black enrollment in public higher education with 8 percent in predominantly white institutions is established for the next three years. In the overall black student enrollment increased emphasis will be on the identification of the "academically better prepared minority student." Special minority recruitment programs will be sponsored by the Medical College of Georgia.

III. *Faculty, Staff, Administration, Governance.* The Board of Regents will continue efforts to increase Blacks at each institution according to earlier plans in nondoctoral positions and in keeping with relevant labor market in doctoral positions. A clearinghouse will be established to assist in this effort and a firm commitment to "affirmative action" is given for every institution in the system.

On the fifteen member Board of Regents were two Blacks. The Plan indicates that Regents have no control over this problem as the Governor appoints and the Senate approves appointments.

IV. *Enhancement of Black Colleges.* Key elements include *Albany State.* Strengthening of key administrative positions will be addressed in the first twenty-four months of the plan's duration which is September 1978-June 1983; a joint Extension & Public Service Program with Albany Junior College; a detailed productivity and management review of each academic program prior to July 1, 1979; coordination of degree programs at Albany Junior College and Albany State to establish the "Ladder Concept"; Special Studies will be expanded at Albany State; higher admissions requirements for teacher education programs in terms of Grade Point Average; upgrading requirements for nursing program; extensive improvements in quality of physical environment; a Distinguished Scholars Program. If significant progress is not made, merger of Albany State and Albany Junior will be considered. *Fort Valley.* Additional staff to include Director of Business Operations and Finance; establishment of a Rural Life Center, with programs indicated above and extensive research activity; a detailed productivity and management review of academic programs; expansion of Special Studies; higher admission requirements for teacher education programs; improvement in physical environment. *Savannah State.* Strengthening administrative positions; a joint Public Service and Extension program with Armstrong State College; higher admission and retention requirements; expansion of Special Studies; one million dollars per year to improve physical environment.

V. *Monitoring/Reporting.* The plan promises the "establishment of a biracial citizens committee to be known as 'the Special Regents' Committee on Desegregation.'" The committee will monitor progress on the plan's implementation. Appropriate reports will be issued by the Board of Regents.

Florida

In 1980 Florida had a total population of 9,739,992 of which 1,342,478 were black. Florida A&M is the one predominately Black university.

One of the original Adams states, Florida filed with the U.S. Department of Health, Education and Welfare a document entitled *A Plan for Equalizing Educational Opportunity in the State University System,* approved by the Board of Regents June 5, 1973.

On November 10, 1973, HEW advised Florida that its Plan was deficient because the Community College System was excluded and it lacked specificity about converting the dual system to a unitary one. On February 15, 1974, Florida presented to

HEW a two volume plan entitled *Plans for Equalizing Educational Opportunities in Public Higher Education in Florida.* HEW informed the State of deficiencies in the Plan on April 17, 1974. Florida's supplement to *Volume I: Special Affirmations and Actions of the Plans for Equalizing Educational Opportunity in Public Higher Education in Florida* was approved by HEW on June 21, 1974. In August 1975, plaintiffs went to court and as a result the Court ordered HEW to require six state (including Florida) to submit new desegregation plans and to set specific standards for those plans. The Court further directed HEW to require each state to submit, within 60 days of receipt of the criteria, a revised desegregation plan and to accept or reject such desegregation plan within 120 days thereafter.

On July 5, 1977, Florida received the HEW criteria, and responded by filing on September 9, 1977, with HEW, a document entitled *Florida's Commitment to Equal Access and Equal Opportunity in Public Higher Education in Florida.* HEW reported to the state that more specific affirmations and measures designed to fulfill the philosophical commitments than indicated in the document just referred to were required.

Florida then submitted two additional documents to HEW—one on October 12, 1977, and amended in January 1978. It is titled *The State University System Revised Plan for Equalizing Educational Opportunity in Public Higher Education in Florida.* The second document, *State Equal Access-Equal Opportunity Plan for the Florida Public Community College System* was submitted on September 12, 1977 and amended in November and December 1977. These two documents along with the *Commitment* paper filed with HEW in September of 1977 make up the Florida Plan for compliance with Title VI. The Plan was approved by Secretary Joseph A. Califano on February 3, 1978.

Because Florida was deemed too slow in implementing the 1978 Plan HEW asked for a new plan. Florida stalled, but the new plan was submitted and approved in April 1981. Approval was based on four documents: (1) February 21, 1981 letter from R. Turlington to F. Croffi forwarding *Florida's Plans for Equal Access and Equal Opportunity in Public Higher Education Response to OCR 1978-79 Evaluations;* (2) February 26, 1981 letter from Commissioner Turlington to F. Croffi at USDOE forwarding *Response of Florida Public Community College System to the January 15 letter and Attachments from Cynthia Brown, Assistant Secre-*

tary for Civil Rights; (3) April 1, 1981, letter and attachments from Chancellor B. Neivell and Commissioner Turlington to F. Croffi; (4) April 15, 1981 letter and enclosure from G. Bedell to F. Croffi with enrollment projections for new programs at Florida A&M University.

The collegiate public education system has two major components: the Community College System; The State University System.

The community colleges are governed by twenty-eight district boards with members approved by the Governor, approved by State Board of Education and confirmed by the Senate. The nine state universities are governed by a single Board of Regents composed of nine voting members and a non-voting student member appointed by the Governor. Regents are appointed and confirmed in the same manner as community college trustees. The State Board of Education comprised of seven elected state officials has general supervisory responsibilities for all public education in Florida. The Department of Education, under supervision of the State Board of Education, is made up of the Commissioner, his staff and five divisions: public schools, vocational education, community colleges, universities, and blind services.

The Division of Community Colleges is headed by a Director, nominated by the Commissioner and appointed by the State Board of Education. The Division of Universities has the Board of Regents at the helm with the Chancellor serving as chief executive officer. The State Board of Education, the Commissioner of Education, and a number of committees and task forces facilitate cooperation between the Community College System and the State University System.

Make-up of the Higher Education System: nine state universities; fourteen off campus centers; twenty-eight community colleges.

Community colleges operate an "open door admissions policy" offering associate degree and certificate programs. Fourteen serve as vocational-technical centers. Community college A.A. graduates are guaranteed access to the upper division level in the State University System.

The State has within its borders three traditionally Black institutions of higher learning. Two are private and one is public. During the Fall of 1976 black students comprised 21 percent of the full-time first year students enrolling in public community colleges.

I. *Disestablishment of the Dual System.* New high demand programs will be placed at Florida A&M University with 40 percent of Florida A & M students in unduplicated programs or high demand programs. Among the new programs will be film and electronic media, landscape design, and respiratory therapy. Unnecessary duplication of programs will be eliminated.

II. *Student Enrollments.* Commitments in this area include open admission not based on race; increased white attendance at FAMU with numerical projections; parity in the proportions of black and white students at all relevant levels, including transfers from community colleges; descriptions of recruitment programs for other race students; special efforts to increase black enrollment at the nine public universities and establishment of retention goals; finding creative approaches to helping students finance their education; increasing the percentage of black student enrollment in graduate and professional schools to approximate black/white proportions receiving Bachelor's degrees within State University System; reduction of racial disparities in retention rates; increased mobility between community colleges and the State University System; education grants to increase black enrollment in graduate fields where blacks have low presence.

III. *Faculty, Staff, Administration, Governance.* For positions not requiring the doctorate making the proportion of black employees approximate the percent of Master's degrees awarded blacks in the State University System in 1975–76 (or 7.6%) is the goal. For community colleges, the goal is 10 percent level of black employment. In positions requiring the doctorate nationwide availability of blacks with appropriate credentials will be the measure. The Plan also includes special upward mobility programs for black employees. In other employment categories the goal is 12.7 percent, the approximate black population of Florida.

IV. *Enhancement of Black University* (Florida A & M University). New Programs. (1) Allied Health Sciences (Medical Records Administration, Physical Therapy, Respiratory Therapy, Health Management). (2) Architecture Technology & Engineering Technology. (3) Landscape Design. (4) Broadcast Engineering. (5) Film Electronic Media. (6) Magazine Production.

Physical facilities at Florida A & M will be improved to achieve comparability between facilities there and at white institutions. Also, funded enrollment capacity at FAMU will be maintained and increased for the duration of the plan.

V. *Monitoring/Reporting.* Responsibilities in this area are assigned to the State Board of Regents' staff and State Community College Division's staff.

Arkansas

Arkansas had a population of 2,285,513 in 1980, with a Black population of 373,192.

Arkansas operates nineteen public institutions of higher education. Only the University of Arkansas—Pine Bluff is a predominantly Black institution. There are nine senior state colleges and universities, 9 state supported two-year institutions, and the University of Arkansas Medical Sciences Campus.

1. Arkansas State University—Jonesboro, Arkansas
2. Arkansas State University—Beebe-Beebe, Arkansas
3. Arkansas Tech University—Russelville, Arkansas
4. Henderson State University—Arkadelphia, Arkansas
5. Southern Arkansas University—Magnolia, Arkansas
6. Southern Arkansas University—El Dorado, Arkansas
7. Southwest Technical Institute—Southern Arkansas University, Camden, Arkansas
8. University of Arkansas at Fayetteville—Fayetteville, Arkansas
9. University of Arkansas at Little Rock—Little Rock Arkansas
10. University of Arkansas at Monticello—Monticello, Arkansas
11. University of Arkansas at Pine Bluff, Arkansas
12. University of Arkansas Medical Sciences Campus—Little Rock, Arkansas
13. University of Central Arkansas—Conway, Arkansas
14. East Arkansas Community College—Forrest City, Arkansas
15. Garland County Community College—Hot Springs, Arkansas
16. Mississippi County Community College—Blytheville, Arkansas
17. North Arkansas Community College—Harrison, Arkansas
18. Phillips County Community College—Helena, Arkansas
19. Westark Community College—Fort Smith, Arkansas

With regard to governance, institutions are divided into 3 major systems: University of Arkansas System; Arkansas State University System; Southern Arkansas University System.

The six community colleges have their own board of trustees.

The University of Arkansas—Pine Bluff has its own special advisory board, which relates to the Board of Trustees for the University of Arkansas. Senior college boards are appointed by the Governor while junior board members are elected in districts where the colleges are located.

The department of Higher Education is the primary action element in higher education governance.

Of significance perhaps is the role Arkansas has played in the desegregation of secondary schools and in admitting blacks to medical and graduate schools. The state was among the first in the South to face desegration at secondary levels in 1957 and among the first to admit a Black to its medical schools, law school, and graduate schools.

I. *Disestablishment of the Structure of the Dual System.* Missions for all institutions are defined without regard to race. All institutions are committed to programs for socially, culturally, educationally, and economically disadvantaged students. These commitments are part of institutional publication content.

Note: Earlier work by Dr. Henry Cobb is acknowledged.

The new programs at University of Arkansas-Pine Bluff are:

Nursing—B.A.

Special Education—B.A.

Psychology—B.A.

Political Science—B.A.

Industrial Technology—A.A.

Law Enforcement—A.A.

Graduate Residence Center for M.Ed. offered by University of Arkansas-Fayetteville

II. *Student Enrollment.* Commitments in this area include: the proportion of black high school graduates entering two-year and four-year institutions of higher education shall be at least equal to the proportion of whites entering; (the Plan points out that this has been virtually achieved in terms of first year enrollments); increasing annually the proportion of black to white undergraduate enrollment in traditionally white four-year public institutions until the disparity between whites and blacks in this category has been eliminated (This would mean 16 percent of such enrollment would be black in 1982-83); parity in the proportions of black and white state students who graduate from public undergraduate institutions in state and enter state graduate and professional schools; increasing the total proportion of whites attending traditionally black institutions; reduce the disparity between percentage of black and white students graduating from the state system; expansion of mobility between community colleges and 4-year colleges.

III. *Desegregation of Faculty, Administration, Staff, Governance.* Recruitment of Blacks for positions not requiring doctorate will be equal to proportion of master's degrees awarded to blacks by Arkansas institutions or percentage of blacks in relevant labor market, whichever is greater; for positions requiring doctorate and nonacademic personnel blacks in relevant labor market is to be the measure.

In instances where Board members are appointed, the goal is increased black representation until black presence reflects black population of state and the area served by the institution.

IV. *Enhancement of Black University.* New academic programs as listed above are committed. Equalization of faculty salaries; upgrading of physical facilities to comparability with other institutions in state; parity in student financial aid funds with other institutions; elimination of educationally unnecessary program duplication between white universities and UAPB not required since no unnecessary duplication exists; priority to be given to UAPB in placement of new high demand programs.

V. *Monitoring/Reporting.* Beginning in August 1978 and each August thereafter the Department of Higher Education will present a report to the Office of Civil Rights to include the following.

1. A description of specific measures taken to achieve objectives enumerated in plan
2. A description of results achieved
3. An analysis of the reason why any steps taken proved inadequate or insufficient
4. A description of steps the state will take to achieve progress and to maintain the time tables set forth in the plan.

The state is committed to provided any statistical reports or other information deemed necessary.

Some Observations and Concerns Regarding Plans Reviewed

On the basis of the review of the six plans selected certain observations and concerns and projections seem reasonable in relationship to the states' responses to HEW criteria in their submissions.

A. Program enhancement at predominantly Black colleges almost always entails the addition of graduate programs and some undergraduate programs in Education. Education is the field in which black presence is highest among master's and doctorate degree holders. Traditional fields in which there is a shortage of blacks seldom appear among the assignments of new programs at predominantly black institutions.

B. Where duplication of programs at proximate institutions is not directly addressed in the plan the black institutions are likely to have difficulty or find it impossible to meet other race student goals. There seems to be considerable variation in the extent to which quantitative goals are present in plans. One factor that might affect this dimension of the plans is the number of black institutions in the state and the black population in the vicinity of the predominantly white institutions.

C. New programs at black institutions provided as means of enhancement have not included doctoral programs in traditional fields but rather in nontraditional, evolving disciplines, where curricula and curricula materials are limited. This, coupled with the dearth of Ph.D's in such fields especially black Ph.Ds. would seem to create problems in those institutions—which are least equipped to deal with them. In the development of high quality programs of graduate study at black institutions, the assignment of traditional mainstay or core curriculum master's and doctoral programs would seem to be imperative.

D. Some programs being placed at predominantly black institutions are high demand offerings but entail certification and accreditation problems. Graduates must pass examinations and programs must be accredited. In Nursing for example graduates of predominantly white institutions in Louisiana are currently experiencing poor performance on national examinations. In future evaluations of these programs poor ratings on passing examinations can be easily cited as basis for eliminating them.

E. Enhancement of black institutions and faculty salary

equalization should be intertwined. Without salary equalization new black doctorates could be attracted to higher salaries at predominantly white institutions while Black institutions are without similar enticement for whites. This situation could yield an imbalance in institutional capability to meet other race faculty goals.

F. The goal of enhancement of black institutions and the goal of attracting white students through high demand programs or non-duplicated programs might be incompatible. Desegregation (attracting white students) could lead to special offerings to meet short term market demands at the expense of developing high quality programs at black institutions.

G. Student Enrollment goals are exceptionally vague in some of the plans. Assessment of success will probably be equally vague. Specific numerical goals would seem imperative.

H. One consideration that might be needed is the fact that while parity in tuition scholarship and support services is provided, the need for aid on the part of black students is usually more severe. Efforts at upgrading black enrollment perhaps ought to be tied to state family income statistics along racial lines. Such a scheme would provide a more realistic measure of relative need.

I. Faculty development at predominantly black institutions does not encompass post-doctoral needs in most plans. Support for completion of terminal degrees seems to be the ultimate, "but the Ph.D is only the beginning." Postdoctoral research, sabattical leaves for course development, and other supports necessary to build quality programs likely to attract able students with options within the state over time seem to be absent.

J. There are no provisions for sabattical leaves to permit thoughtful, insightful, and careful planning activities in the development of new programs at the predominantly black institutions. If these programs are to be well developed, with adquate study of financial and academic needed, curricula building and the like, longer time periods for preparing proposals will be needed. In at least one case, overloaded faculty have been faced with the responsibility for submitting comprehensive plans for nontraditional programs in 2–4 weeks without opportunity to leave their own campuses or to have input from consultants. Consultant input is needed and there is also a need to evaluate that input and adjust it to needs of the affected institutions.

K. Monitoring and Reporting components of the plans provide different levels of input for interested parties. Where State higher education officials have exclusive control over the process the results might be different from situations where Black institutions/groups or citizens have some input. Also, where both narrative and statistical reports are required the assessment process is likely to be more informative than where only 1 type of report is required.

Possible Variables for a Political Taxonomy

Any discussion aimed at classifying the patterns offered by states for desegregating their systems of higher education would seem to necessitate consideration of several factors. Some of these factors and justifications for suggesting them are included in this section.

A. The method by which the plan was developed. Differences in plans will perhaps be partially a result of whether the means of developing plans was by: court order; negotiations between the Office of Civil Rights and states; consent decree involving OCR, the state and the Department of Justice; or by voluntary, unsolicited submissions from the state.

B. The Date of the Plan or settlement. Plans negotiated prior to 1981 are likely to differ from those completed in 1980 or earlier due to the changing dynamics of the national political scene.

C. Nature of traditional race relations in the State. States characterized by less volatile traditional race relations are likely to end up with plans that differ from states with a history of more traumatic, conflictual race relations.

D. Proportion of blacks in the population of the state. States with relatively large proportions of blacks in the population (28% or more) are likely to have responded differently to the desegregation challenge than those with small black proportions.

E. Comparative literacy levels for whites and blacks in the

state population. Levels of college attendance and support for higher education are likely to be affected by literacy levels and therefore the nature of the plans is likely to be affected.

F. Number of predominantly black institutions in the State. The financial outlay entailed in enhancement of black institutions will be affected by the number. States with only one black institution are likely to respond differently from those with two or more black colleges.

G. Extent of disparity between proportion of black high school graduates attending college and white graduates attending. The magnitude of the disparity will affect the kind of effort (financial, structural, and programmatic) needed to meet federal guidelines, and this is likely to be reflected in state plans.

H. Number, status, and reputation of predominantly white institutions. At least three groups of institutions emerge—predominantly white "Flagship" institution(s); other white institutions; and predominantly black institutions. The total number of white institutions competing for state funds becomes a major factor in settlement efforts since enhancement of black institutions will entail financial resources that would otherwise go to white institutions.

I. Number of boards of governance involved in negotiations. Outcomes of negotiations will likely be affected by the number of boards having input in the process. Especially significant is whether a board of governance of black institutions is involved.

J. Presence of blacks on boards of governance. Black presence on boards of governance could impact outcome of negotiations based on the percentage of total membership they constitute.

K. Role of governor and other political elites in the negotiations. In at least one state the governor took personal charge of the negotiations and made public statements advocating several positions. This kind of involvement almost certainly affects the outcome of negotiations.

L. Proportion of blacks attending predominantly white institutions at time of plan and the configuration of black participation at those institutions (athletics and other activities). The degree to which black presence is already a reality at white institutions will almost certainly be a factor in negotiations.

M. Role of the NAACP and other groups outside of the education system. Groups not accountable to the coordinating authority for higher education in the state can play a crucial role in negotiations because of their independence. NAFEO's role was especially important in the *Adams* cases.

N. Status of black political participation in the state. The extent to which blacks hold political office, especially state legislative positions, will probably impact the status of the plan.

O. Geographic location of black and white institutions in relationship to each other. Whether black and white institutions are in close proximity is *one* of the major factors affecting the content of state plans.

P. The nature of the monitoring/reporting scheme. Implementation of plans and monitoring/reporting schemes are likely to be intertwined.

Q. Role of the federal government in the settlement/plan. Nature of the guidelines offered by the federal government and the extent to which the federal government was involved in actual negotiations will influence the plan.

R. Role of "informal agreements" or understandings that may be attached to particular officeholders. Whether such agreements will outlive the tenure of those around whom they were negotiated will be a factor in implementation.

This listing is certainly not meant to be exhaustive but would seem to suggest major variables that could serve as the impetus for developing a political taxonomy of desegregating higher education.

4 Constitutional Requirements

Paul R. Dimond

Despite the rising tide of antisegregation law loosed by *Brown*, there has been relatively little case law and commentary concerning desegregation of higher education. Moreover, the trickle of writing and argument on the issue is couched more in terms of policy reactions to perceived problems than in terms of how general principles of constitutional law and equitable remedy should be applied to particular systems of higher education in specific states. Commentators and courts apparently feel that higher education is so unique that it deserves a law of its own or fear that the even-handed application of otherwise applicable remedial doctrine leads to results that are politically difficult to achieve and socially difficult to swallow.
desegregation of higher education seems so infected by this malaise that it results in attempts to "balance" competing social concerns and constituencies without the benefit of *any* guiding constitutional objective.

It is difficult to make much legal sense out of various "balancing" arguments that seek to address questions like "What do we do about the black colleges?" and "What amount of desegregation of predominantly black and white schools is enough?" rather than questions like "What is the general constitutional rule for overcoming any continuing effects of prior forced segregation," "How can full access to higher education be guaranteed for minorities previously excluded altogether or segregated in higher education?" and "How should these principles be applied to formerly dual systems of higher education in the particular circumstances of each state?" As a result, this paper will not address the various "balancing" arguments that have dominated the higher education desegregation debate for the past decade. It will not discuss the merits of OCRs 2 February 1978 "criteria" nor the recent "settlements" in North Carolina and

Louisiana; such discussion would inevitably lead to policy disputes that obscure rather than inform the basic legal issue. Instead, two constitutional legal principles for understanding the wrong of official racial discrimination and providing a commensurate remedy will be posed (Part B, *infra*), their historical development described (Part C, *infra*), and their application to higher education explored (Part D, *infra*).

Generally Applicable Constitutional Principles

The first constitutional rule is that a state that has in the past restricted access to higher education on a racial basis—by exclusion of blacks from particular whites-only colleges or graduate institutions altogether—bears the affirmative duty to insure that black applicants who can benefit from higher education are no longer effectively excluded. This is a principle of meaningful access for individual blacks who aspire to higher education and possess the requisite qualifications or potential. The second constitutional rule is that a state that has in the past imposed mandatory segregation in its system of higher education bears the affirmative duty to implement a plan of actual desegregation that, subject to the practicalities of the local situation, (a) will work to convert to a unitary system without "black schools" or "white schools" but "just schools," (b) realistically begins through appropriate ancillary relief to overcome any residual effects of the former dual schooling, and (c) does not pick disproportionately on identifiably black as compared to white interests to bear the brunt of any remedial burdens. This is a principle of group relief from class segregation. Both of these rules assume a constitutional violation requiring affirmative relief rather than racial neutrality that would freeze-in the violation.

Neither of these two principles recognizes any "vested right" in historically black or white colleges and universities. Although the state may have made one institution or another *objectively* better or worse if it has funded schools based on white supremacy stereotypes, historic black schools are not *inherently* inferior because predominantly black nor white schools *inherently* superior because predominantly white. As a result, particular institutions, do have interests and qualities that the state may (and, in some instances, must) consider (along with other interests) in developing and choosing between alternative remedies that promise to work. But people, not buildings or schools, have constitutional rights; and states have duties to afford constitutional protection to their citizens.

In my opinion, the important constitutional issue that must be resolved is whether only the access rule or also the principle of group relief now apply to any state's higher education system. Decision will turn on (a) whether the evidence in a particular case concerning the nature and extent of the violation prove that the current racial duality between historically white and black schools results in fact from the continuing effects of the original violation (rather than the intervening, independent choice of students, staff, and administrators), and (b) whether, in any event, the arguably voluntary nature of higher education permits application of *only* the access but not the group relief analysis. The basic issue must finally be faced (not ducked by the diverse *ad hoc* "balancing" claims) if the Constitution rather than politics is ever to provide guidance in explaining what "desegregation" of higher education means. In order to understand this question, Part C will trace the development of two constitutional principles; and Part D will explore their application to higher education. The paper will conclude with an attempt to resolve the basic constitutional issue.

Historical Development of Desegregation Standards

Pre-Brown Understanding of the Constitutional Wrong

In the *Dred Scott* case, 60 U.S. (19 How.) 393 (1857), Chief Justice Taney wrote blacks entirely out of the definition of a "citizen" under the United States Constitution. In this pernicious judgment, *all* blacks (including "free blacks") were viewed as "beings of an inferior order . . . altogether unfit to associate with the white race . . . an ordinary article of merchandise. . . . This stigma, of deepest degradation, was fixed upon the whole race." 60 U.S. at 407, 410. The opinion justified the exclusion of black people from the fundamental social contract of the nation because all Negroes, in Taney's view of the Framers' intent, were "at that time considered as a subordinate and inferior class of beings, who had been subjugated by the dominant race and, whether emancipated or not, yet remained subject to their authority . . . " 60 U.S. at 404–5.

This blatant admission of the wrong of racism in America—a caste system officially implying white superiority and dominance and black inferiority and servility—was in the eyes of some the fundamental point of attack for the post-Civil War amendments and civil rights statutes of 1866, 1870, 1871, and 1875. *One* way to describe the ensuing post-Reconstruction opinions of the Supreme Court, then, is a process through which a majority of the Justices slowly but surely limited what racially discriminatory actions would be considered to carry such stigmatizing connotations. That process served to legitimize and fuel Jim Crow segregation laws throughout much of the nation and to ratify no less effective customary segregation and discrimination throughout all of the country.

In *Strauder* v. *West Virginia*, 100 U.S. 303 (1880), a case challenging whites-only juries, however, the Court first held that the 14th Amendment "is one of a series of constitutional provisions having a common purpose, namely: securing to a race recently emancipated, a race that had been held in slavery, all the civil rights that the superior race enjoy . . ." As a result, the 14th Amendment was read as securing a positive immunity or right "to the colored race—the right to exemption from unfriendly legislation against them distinctively as colored; exemption from legal discriminations, implying inferiority in civil society, lessening the security of their enjoyment of the rights which others enjoy, and discriminations which are steps towards reducing them to the condition of a subject race." 100 U.S. at 307-308. Based on this understanding of the meaning of the 14th Amendment, the Court found that the exclusion of blacks from jury service violated the 14th Amendment: "The very fact that colored people are singled out and expressly denied by a statute all right to participate in the administration of the law, as jurors, because of their color . . . is practically a brand upon them, affixed by the law; an assertion of their inferiority, and a stimulant to that race prejudice which is an impediment to securing to individuals of the race that equal justice which the law aims to secure to all others." 100 U.S. at 308.

Three years later in the *Civil Rights Cases*, 109 U.S. 3 (1883), the Court severely restricted what discriminations would be deemed stigmatizing attempts to place the Freedmen in a position of inferiority in violation of the 13th and 14th Amendments. In declaring unconstitutional that portion of the 1875 Civil Rights Act which made it unlawful to discriminate against blacks in inns, theaters, and conveyances, the majority held that such "quasi-public" places did not amount to the "state action" which the Court supposed to be required under the 14th Amendment, 109 U.S. at 16-19; and that, although Congress had the power under the 13th Amendment "to pass all laws necessary and proper for abolishing all badges and incidents of slavery in the United States," 109 U.S. at 20, the private act of the innkeeper in excluding blacks "has nothing to do with slavery or involuntary servitude . . . [The discriminatee's] redress [if any] is to be sought [solely] under the laws of the State." 109 U.S. at 24. Looking to the second-class status of "*free* colored people in this country before the abolition of slavery" for his justification for this startling revelation, Justice Bradley opined that "mere" discriminations on account of race or color were not regarded as "badges of slavery." 109 U.S. at 25.

Justice Harlan dissented. He argued that the majority's "state action" bar was a fabrication to protect public and customary discrimination from redress. 109 U.S. at 43-60. Harlan also found that racial discrimination in places otherwise open to the public amounted to a badge or incident of slavery: "since slavery . . . was the moving or principal cause Bf the adoption of the [13th] Amendment, and since that institution rested wholly upon the inferiority, as a race, of those held in bondage, their freedom necessarily involved immunity from, and protection against, all discrimination against them, because of their race, in respect of such civil rights as belong to freemen of other races." 109 U.S. at 36. Thus, for example, Harlan found "locomotion" was necessary for full freedom and that racial discrimination in public conveyances is one of the "burdens which lie at the very foundation of the institution of slavery as it once existed. They are not to be sustained, except upon the assumption that there is, in this land of universal liberty, a class which may still be discriminated against . . . [A] freeman is not only thereby branded as one inferior and infected but . . . is robbed of some of the essential means of existence; and all this solely because they belong to a particular race, which the nation has liberated." 109 U.S. at 39-40. Justice Bradley, speaking for the majority, retorted: "It would be running the slavery argument into the ground to make it apply to every act of discrimination which a person may see fit to make as to the guests he will entertain, or as to the people he will take into his coach or cab or car . . . " 109 U.S. at 24.

Frederick Douglass was the fugitive slave who had led the fight for abolition of slavery from the South *and* for full freedom for "free" blacks excluded, segregated, and ostracized throughout the rest of the nation. He had long argued vehemently against racial restrictions in any civic, community, or other facility generally open to the public such as those condoned in *Civil Rights Cases*. With respect to segregated schools, Douglass added: "We want mixed schools not because our colored schools are inferior—not because colored instructors are inferior to white instructors—but because we want to do away with a system that exalts one class and debases another." For Douglass, "If there is no struggle, there is no progress. Those who profess to favor freedom, and yet deprecate agitation, are men who want crops without plowing up the ground. Power concedes nothing without a demand." Yet the Hayes-Tilden compromise in the 1876 presidential election withdrew federal oversight of civil rights in the South, and the decision in the *Civil Rights Cases* placed customary discrimination and community segregation beyond the Civil War Amendments. The end of Reconstruction and the reign of unchallenged white supremacy and caste relations was at hand. In 1895 Frederick Douglass died, and Booker T. Washington, the President of Tuskegee Institute, sought to reach a mode of practical survival for blacks in the increasingly hostile environment. At the Atlanta Exposition, he stressed the need for vocational training and common labor for his race as the best means of selfhelp. If whites would accept this accommodation, blacks would "stand by [whites] with a devotion that no foreigner can approach, ready to lay down our lives in defense of yours, interlacing our industrial, commercial, civil, and religious life with yours in a way that shall make the interests of both races one. In all things that are purely social can be as separate as the fingers, yet one as the hand in all things essential to mutual progress." He concluded that "the wisest among my race understands that the agitation of questions of social equality is the extremest folly, and that progress in the enjoyment of all the privileges that will come to us must be the result of severe and constant struggle rather than artificial forcing." Washington may have spoken of accommodation, but his white listeners heard the words of surrender.

The Supreme Court greeted Washington's call the next year by completing the process of legitimizing racial discrimination in *Plessy* v. *Ferguson* (1896). The crux of the majority's opinion is contained in the following three sentences:

> [If] the enforced separation of the two races stamps the colored with a badge of inferiority . . . , it is not by reason of anything found in the act, but solely because the colored race chooses to put that construction upon it. The plaintiff's argument necessarily assumes that if, as has been more than once the case, and is not unlikely to be so again, the colored race should become the dominant power in the state legislature, and should enact a law in precisely similar terms, it would thereby relegate the white race to an inferior position. We imagine that the white race, at least, would not acquiesce in this assumption.

163 U.S. 537, 551-552 (1896). As Prof. Black so aptly described these sentences in his defense of *Brown* from attack by Prof. Wechsler, "the curves of callousness and stupidity intersect at their respective maxima." *See*, C. Black, "The Lawfulness of the Segregation Decisions," 69 Yale L. J. 421 (1960).

The *Plessy* majority further opined that "if one race be inferior to the other socially, the Constitution of the United States cannot put them on the same plane." The *Plessy* majority even put the lie to its own deceitful logic by reserving to the states damage actions for "white" persons wrongly excluded from the "whites-only" coach because mistakenly accused of being "colored." With respect to the criminal indictment against Homer Plessy, an octaroon who could pass for white but challenged mandatory segregation in railroad cars instead, the court reserved a similar racial defense for the trial:

> [T]he question of the proportion of colored blood necessary to constitute a colored person, as distinguished from a white person, is one on which there is a difference of opinion . . . [I]t may undoubtedly become a question of importance whether, under the laws of Louisiana, [Plessy] belongs to the white or colored race.

163 U.S. at 552. The Court merely ignored Plessy's plea for freedom from such stigmatization, ostracism, and forced segregation:

> [I]t is not of the smallest consequence that the car or compartment set apart for the Colored is "equal" in those incidents which affect physical comfort to that set apart for the Whites. These might even be superior. . . . The White man's wooden railway benches, if the case were such, would be preferred to any velvet cushions in the Colored car. If Mr. Plessy be Colored, and has tasted of the advantages of free American citizenship, and has responded to its inspirations, he abhorred the equal accommodations of the car to which he was compulsorily assigned!

Although Justice Harlan subsequently gave sway to separate *and* unequal in *Cumming* v. *Richmond County Board of Education*, 175 U.S. 528 (1899), the majority's lies in *Plessy* were too much. "Everyone knows that the statute in question had its origin in the purpose . . . to exclude colored people from coaches occupied by or assigned to white persons . . . The thing to accomplish was, under the guise of giving equal accommodations for white and blacks, to compel the latter to keep to themselves. . . . No one would be so wanting in candor as to assert the contrary." Relying on notions of personal freedom and association inhering in his view of the 13th and 14th Amendments, 163 U.S. at 555-569, Harlan prophetically concluded that the majority's judgment "will, in time, prove to be quite as pernicious as the decision made by this tribunal in the *Dred Scott Case*:"

> What can more certainly arous race hate, what more certainly create and perpetuate a feeling of mistrust between the races, than state enactments which in fact proceed on the ground that colored citizens are so inferior and degraded that they cannot be allowed to sit in public coaches occupied by white citizens? That, as all will admit, is the real meaning of such legislation as was enacted in Louisiana.

163 U.S. at 560. For Harlan, "the arbitrary separation of the citizens, on the basis of race, while they are on a public highway, is a badge of servitude wholly inconsistent with civil freedom and the equality before the law established by the Constitution." 163 U.S. at 561–562.

In 1908, the Court completed its validation of forced segregation by approving Kentucky's prohibition of any interacial association, even if the result of voluntary choice of blacks and whites alike in attending private colleges. *Berea College* v. *Kentucky*, 211 U.S. S. 45 (1908). Separate and unequal segregation in virtually all affairs had become the American way of life. It replaced slavery as the vehicle to perpetuate racial caste, to deprive individual blacks of personal freedom and access to all variety of opportunity for a full life, and to discriminate against all blacks as a group by stigmatizing them as an inherently inferior and undeserving class compared to the dominant white majority. In this context, dual systems of higher education can be understood as one more facet of the pervasive Jim Crow segregation that divided the country on a racial basis. Consistent with this understanding, the States sought to limit the mission of the black institutions to training blacks as teachers for blacks-only schools and as laborers on the white man's farm or mechanics in the white man's field, while white colleges and universities were supported to advance a full range of human learning, profession, and activity.

This color line, and Booker T. Washington's counsel of accommodation, did not long go unchallenged. W.E.B. Du Bois published *The Souls of Black Folk* in 1903. He wrote:

> So far as Mr. Washington preaches Thrift, Patience, and Industrial Training for the Masses, we must hold up our hands and strive with him. . . . But so far as Mr. Washington apologizes for injustice, North or South, does not rightly value the privilege and duty of voting, belittles the emasculating effects of caste distinctions, and opposes the higher training and ambition of our brighter minds—so far as he, the South, or the Nation, does this—we must increasingly and firmly oppose them.

Du Bois took similar aim at segregation:

> The problem of the twentieth century is the problem of the color line. . . . Negroes are a segregated and servile caste with restricted rights and privileges. . . . The hands of none of us are clean if we bend not our energies to righting these great wrongs.

By 1905 Du Bois joined with others to form the Niagra Movement dedicated to "aggressive action" to secure black freedom: "We refuse to allow the impression to remain that the Negro-American assents to inferiority, [or] is submissive under oppression. . . . We will not be satisfied to take one jot or tittle less than our . . . full rights." By 1909 a bi-racial coalition formed the NAACP, and Du Bois became its spokesman through monthly publication of *The Crisis*. In the battle for black aspiration, Du Bois prevailed with his call for full freedom over Washington's plan for accommodation, even if most blacks did the best they could in their daily striving while living under the continuing yoke of Jim Crow segregation.

Over the next decades, the Supreme Court began to erode, to limit, or even to ignore the worst implications of *Plessy* v. *Ferguson* in cases concerning racial zoning (*Buchanan* v. *Warley*), grandfather voting clauses (*U.S.* v. *Guinn* and *Lane* v. *Wilson*), white primaries (*Smith* v. *Allwright*), and restrictive covenants (*Shelly* v. *Kramer*). But the forced separation of *Plessy*, without even the appearance of equality, still dominated most public facilities and community affairs.

By 1930, the NAACP determined to mount a legal campaign to attack the underbelly of the separate-but-equal doctrine: segregation, as then provided and administered, expended from two to ten times as many dollars per white pupil as per black pursuant to Jim Crow laws and practices that habitually failed to guarantee the equal facilities mandated by *Plessy*. In implementing this strategy, Charles Houston, the NAACP's first General Counsel, determined to attack higher education where (with the exception of Meharry Medical College) there were *no* graduate or professional schools open to any black in the South. To maintain this color line under *Plessy's* separate but equal command, the States would have to build separate black graduate schools or include blacks on a segregated (and even more blatantly discriminatory) basis within otherwise white schools. At a minimum, separate education for blacks would be vastly improved by expanding the mission of black colleges; at a maximum, the discrimination inherent in forced separation would be exposed at the highest levels of American life and learning. This strategy also appealed to the increasingly frustrated Du Bois who left the NAACP because of his fear that racial bias ran so deep in the white majority (a) that discrimination would play its evil hand on innocent black youth in ostensibly mixed institutions dominated by whites and (b) that ending segregation might only mean the disbanding of black institutions and culture altogether.

In the first of the higher education cases to reach the Supreme Court, Lloyd Gaines had applied to the whites-only Missouri law school rather than accept an offer of tuition to attend an out-of-state school or wait until the blacks-only Lincoln University builB a comparable law school. By a 6-2 vote, the Court ruled that the options afforded Gaines were insufficient to meet the State's duty to treat its black and white students equally. Lloyd Gaines' "right was a personal one. It was as an individual that he was entitled to the equal protection of the laws, and the State was bound to furnish him within its borders facilities for legal education substantially equal to those which the State there afforded for persons of the White race, whether or not other Negroes sought the same opportunity." *Missouri ex rel. Gaines* v. *Canada*, 305 U.S. 337, 351 (1938). Gaines was therefore entitled to be admitted "to the law school of the State University in the absence of other and proper provision for his legal training within the State." 305 U.S. at 352. Justice McReynolds dissented:

> For a long time Missouri has acted upon the view that the best interest of her people demands separation of whites and negroes in schools. Under the opinion just announced, I presume she may abandon her law school and thereby disadvantage her white citizens without improving [Gaines'] opportunities for legal instruction; or she may break down the settled practice concerning separate schools and thereby, as indicated by experience, damnify both races. Whether by some other course it may be possible for her to avoid condemnation is a matter for conjecture.

305 U.S. at 353.

Yet ten years after the *Gaines* decision there were in the South (a) no black universities with graduate schools comparable in quality to white schools and (b) no meaningful access for blacks to traditionally white colleges, universities, and graduate schools. In 1948 Ada Lois Sipuel, a graduate of the State College for Negroes, applied to the University of Oklahoma Law School and, with assistance from NAACP's general counsel Thurgood Marshall, sought to prove that she was entitled to immediate admission rather than to wait for the opening of a black law school that would be inferior in material respects to the established white school. Marshall also offered proof suggesting that a separate black education, cut off from the white mainstream and connections, could not in any event offer an education equal to an established law school. Citing *Gaines*, the Supreme Court tersely ruled that Sipuel was "entitled to secure legal education afforded by a state institution" immediately. *Sipuel* v. *Board of Regents*, 332 U.S. 631, 632 (1948). Oklahoma responded By cordoning off a small section of the State capitol and assigning three teachers to instruct Sipuel and any other black law school applicants. The Supreme Court refused to disturb this dodge, and Sipuel got neither an equal black law school nor the end of exclusively white graduate and professional schools.

Undaunted, Marshall pressed cases on behalf of Herman Sweatt's attempt to breach the whites-only walls of the University of Texas Law School and of George McLaurin's desire to secure a doctorate in education at the University of Oklahoma. The lower court in the Texas case held that Sweatt was not entitled to admission at the whites-only school because the State would provide substantially equivalent facilities at a new black law school. In Oklahoma, the State offered a different gambit: it admitted McLaurin to the previously whites-only university but on a segregated basis, with a separate seat in the cafeteria, classrooms and library; and the trial court refused to enjoin this blatant discrimination.

On appeal, the Supreme Court ruled that the new law school for blacks in Texas did not provide substantial equality of educational opportunity for Sweatt compared to that offered whites at the prestigious Texas Law School in Austin:

> In terms of number of the faculty, variety of courses and opportunity for specialization, size of the student body, scope of the library, availability of law review and similar activities, the University of Texas Law School is superior. What is more important, the University of Texas Law School possesses to a far greater degree those qualities which are incapable of objective measurement but which make for greatness in a law school. Such qualities, to name a few, include reputation of the faculty, experience of the administration, position and influence of the alumni, standing in the community, traditions and prestige. It is difficult to believe that one who had a free choice between these law schools would consider the question close.

The Court continued:

> Moreover, although the law is a highly learned profession, we are well aware that it is an intensely practical one. The law school, the proving ground for legal earning and practice, cannot be effective in isolation from the individuals and institutions with which the law interacts. Few students and no one who has practiced law would choose to study in an academic vacuum, removed from the interplay of ideas and the exchange of views with which the law is concerned. The [black] law school to which Texas is willing to admit [Sweatt] excludes from its student body members of the racial groups which number 85% of the population of the State and include most of the lawyers, witnesses, jurors, judges and other officials with whom [he] will inevitably be dealing when he becomes a member of the Texas Bar. With such a substantial and significant segment of society excluded, we cannot conclude that the education offered [him] is substantially equal to that which he would receive if admitted to the University of Texas Law School.

Sweatt v. *Painter*, 339 U.S. 629, 633, 634 (1950). Given the personal nature of Sweatt's right to a substantially equal opportunity to secure a legal education, the Court held that he was entitled to immediate admission to the University of Texas Law School.

In the Oklahoma case, the Supreme Court held that the State's imposition of racial restrictions on McLaurin's study:

> sets [him] apart from the other students. The result is that [McLaurin] is handicapped in his pursuit of effective graduate instruction. Such restrictions impair and inhibit his ability to study, to engage in discussions and exchange views with other students, and, in general, to learn his profession.
>
> Our society grows increasingly complex, and our need for trained leaders increases correspondingly. [McLaurin's] case represents, perhaps, the epitome of that need, for he is attempting to obtain an advanced degree in education, to become by definition, a leader and trainer of others. Those who will come under his guidance and influence must be directly affected by the education he receives. Their own education and development will necessarily suffer to the extent that his training is unequal to that of his classmates. State-imposed restrictions which produce such inequalities cannot be sustained.

McLaurin v. *Oklahoma State Regents*, 339 U.S. 637, 641 (1950). The State, under the equal protection clause, could not impose racial barriers "which prohibit the intellectual commingling of students . . ." *Id.*

Jim Crow segregation and the separate-but-equal doctrine had not yet fallen, but they were now at least under heavy scrutiny any time a single black individual with the requisite training and credentials might seek to enter a whites-only preserve. In addition, the inquiry into "intangible factors" suggested that the class or group nature of the Jim Crow caste system of discrimination was also open to challenge.

The testing ground for Marshall's assault then shifted to elementary and secondary education. After years of trial work in several cases throughout the Southern and border States, then argument and reargument in the Supreme Court, the decision of *Brown* v. *Board of Education* in 1954 finally answered the big lie of the separate-but-equal doctrine. Writing for a unanimous Court, Chief Justice Warren held:

> To separate [black children in public schools] from others of similar age and qualifications solely because of their race generates a feeling of inferiority as to their status in the community that may affect their hearts and minds in a way unlikely ever to be undone . . . [T]he policy of separating the races is usually interpreted as denoting the inferiority of the Negro group . . . Any language in *Plessy* v. *Ferguson* contrary to this finding is rejected. We conclude that in the field of

> public education the doctrine of "separate but equal" has no place. Separate educational facilities are inherently unequal.

347 U.S. 483, 493–494 (1955). Although the famous (or infamous) footnote 11 cites "social science" evidence in support of this proposition, the *per curiam* decisions following *Brown* that invalidated compulsory segregation statutes in all governmental activities suggest that the Court recognized the stigma of implied racial inferiority inhering in Jim Crow segregation both more broadly and less directly than in the particular motivation and achievement of black school children attending blacks-only schools.

Thus, Professor Charles Black noted that state-imposed segregation was (a) a massive intentional disadvantaging of the black race, as such, by state law, and (b) an integral part of "white supremacy," in "apostolic succession from slavery and the *Dred Scott* case" and the Black Codes, 69 Yale L. J. at 424:

> If a whole race of people finds itself confined within a system which is set up and continued for the very purpose of keeping it in an inferior station, and if the question is then solemnly propounded whether such a race is being treated "equally," I think we ought to exercise one of the sovereign prerogatives of the philosophers—that of laughter.

It takes no seer to perceive that segregation "is a means of ghettoizing the imputedly inferior race." 69 Yale L. J. at 424 n. 25.

Seen in this perspective, *Brown* is a decision outlawing racial discrimination against blacks as a group that happened to involve public schooling, not a decision guaranteeing "equal educational opportunity" (however defined) that happened to involve racial segregation. Nevertheless, controversy continued over whether the constitutional wrong involved only denial of access for individual blacks to otherwise white institutions or also the entire system of group segregation. Genuine free choice might provide individual access for blacks seeking to enter white schools, but only more fundamental restructuring would remedy the caste system of segregated schooling. *Brown II*, whatever its other implications for inordinate delay, confirmed that *both* the individual access and group discrimination aspects were part of the violation: "At stake is the *personal* interest of the plaintiffs in admission for public schools as soon as practicable on a non-discriminatory basis," while the long-term goal was "to effectuate a transition to a racially non-discriminatory school system." 349 U.S. 294, 300–301 (1955). Indeed, the Court permitted delay in order to give the States time to plan and to implement a fundamental restructuring of dual systems of schooling. *Id*.

Post-Brown Desegregation Standards for Elementary and Secondary Education

For years, however, even simple access for blacks who wished to transfer to white schools was in doubt as a result of massive resistance. *See*, e.g., *Cooper* v. *Aaron*, 358 U.S. 1 (1958) and *Griffin* v. *County School Board of Prince Edwards County*, 377 U.S. 218 (1964). Gradually, statements of the fundamental meaning of *Brown* made by the preeminent judges on the lower courts began to reject "free choice" remedies that failed to dismantle dual systems of elementary and secondary education. For example, Judge Wisdom in *United States* v. *Jefferson County Board of Education*, 372 F.2d 836 (5th Cir. 1966), rejected Judge Parker's dictum in *Briggs* v. *Elliott*, 132 F. Supp. 776 (D.S. Car. 1955), that the Constitution requires open access, does not require integration, and does not prohibit voluntary racial choice by individuals of state-supported segregated schools. Wisdom argued that *Brown* recognized the "right of Negroes to *national* citizenship. *Brown* erased *Dred Scott* [and] used the Fourteenth Amendment to breathe life into the Thirteenth . . . Freedmen are freemen . . . No longer 'beings of an inferior race'—the *Dred Scott* article of faith—Negroes too are part of the people of the United States." 372 F.2d at 872. Thus the State's duty is to provide "educational opportunities free of any compulsion that Negroes wear a badge of slavery." 372 F.2d at 873.[1] The State could meet that duty only by fully desegregating the schools:

> Here, school boards, utilizing the dual zoning system, assigned Negro teachers to Negro schools and selected Negro neighborhoods as suitable areas in which to locate Negro schools. Of course, the con-

1. *See also* Judge Sobeloff's similar understanding of *Brown* as expressed in *Brunson* v. *Board of Trustees*, 429 F.2d 820, 826 (4th Cir. 1970) (the lineal descendant of *Briggs*) to reject the "white majority" defense to desegregation in a majority black county school system: "[Desegregation] is not founded upon the concept that white children are a precious resource which should be fairly apportioned. It is not because black children will be improved by their association with their [alleged] betters . . . But school segregation is forbidden precisely because its perpetuation is a living insult to the black children and immeasureably taints the education they receive. This is the precise lesson of *Brown*."

> centration of Negroes increased in the neighborhood of the school. Cause and effect came together. In this circuit, therefore, the location of Negro schools with Negro facilities in Negro neighborhoods and white schools in white neighborhoods . . . came into existence as state action and continues to exist as racial gerrymandering.

372 F.2d at 876.

Similarly, Judge Butzner rejected "free choice" in *Brewer* v. *School Board of the City of Norfolk*, 397 F.2d 37 (4th Cir. 1968). He noted: "This system [of one race facilities and pupil 'choice'] tends to perpetuate a dual system of schools when the identity of Negro and white schools, located in the same zone, can be determined by the racial composition of faculties." 397 F.2d at 39. Judge Butzner took only a slightly different approach than Judge Wisdom to the affirmative duty to desegregate:

> Upon remand the district court should determine whether the racial pattern of the [geographic planning units used by the school administrators to draw zones] results from racial discrimination with regards to housing. If residential racial discrimination exists, it is immaterial that it results from private action. The school board cannot build its exclusionary attendance areas upon private racial discrimination. Assignment of pupils to neighborhood schools is a sound concept, but it cannot be approved if residence in a neighborhood is denied to Negro pupils solely on the ground of color.

397 F.2d at 41–42.

Fourteen years after *Brown*, the Supreme Court finally entered the remedial thicket to answer again whether the Constitutional wrong included the caste system of segregating a group, as well as denial of access to individuals. Speaking for a unanimous Court, Justice Brennan rejected any "free choice" and "free transfer" schemes that perpetuated the basic dual system in a rural, two-school district in which residential segregation caused none of the school segregation:

> The pattern of separate "white" and "Negro" schools in the New Kent County school system established under compulsion of state laws is precisely the pattern of segregation to which *Brown I* and *II* were particularly addressed and which *Brown I* declared unconstitutionally denied Negro school children equal protection of the laws. Racial identification of the system's schools was complete, extending not just to the composition of student bodies but to every facet of school operations—faculty, staff, transportation, extracurricular activities and facilities. In short, the State, acting through

the local school board and school officials, organized and operated a dual system, part "white" and part "Negro."

Green v. *County School Board*, 391 U.S. 430, 435 (1968). Brennan continued:

[The] deliberate perpetuation of the unconstitutional dual system can only have compounded the harm.

391 U.S. at 438. Brennan concluded:

The Board must be required to formulate a new plan . . . and fashion steps which promise realistically to convert to a system without a "white" school and a "Negro" school, but just schools.

391. U.S. at 443.

In the companion case of *Monroe* v. *Board of Education*, the Court applied the same reasoning to reject "free transfers" from zoned assignments as an adequate remedy in a city of 40,000 persons, that resulted in eight "white" schools and five "Negro" schools, with the one-third black population concentrated in the center of the city. 391 U.S. 450, 455–458. In a pointed footnote at the end of the opinion, 391 U.S. at 460 (emphasis supplied), the Court suggested that the plaintiffs' proposal of a feeder system "is an effective alternative, reasonably available to [the school board] to abolish the *dual system* in junior high schools." Group relief from caste segregation, not just open access for individuals, was the Constitutional meaning of "desegregation" for elementary and secondary education.

The only remaining issue for elementary and secondary school desegregation seemed to be whether residential segregation in larger urban areas could be invoked as a limit on the group relief command to desegregate schools. *Jones* v. *Mayer*, 392 U.S. 409 (1968), suggested that continuing residential segregation was also as much an instrument of caste as dual systems of schooling. Justice Stewart speaking for the Court (Harlan and White dissenting on grounds of statutory interpretation), read the 1866 Civil Rights Act to bar discrimination in the private sale of real estate. Stewart argued that the purpose of the 13th Amendment and 42 U.S. §1982 (and by implication the 14th Amendment) included prohibition of caste segregation:

Just as the Black Codes enacted after the Civil War to restrict the free exercise of those rights were substitutes for the slave system, so the exclusion of Negroes from white communities became a substi-

> tute for the Black Codes. And when racial discrimination herds men into ghettos and makes their ability to buy property turn on the color of their skin, then it too is a relic of slavery . . . If Congress cannot say that being a free man means at least this much, then the Thirteenth Amendment made a promise the Nation cannot keep.

392 U.S. at 441–443. Justice Harlan in dissent (joined by White) suggested that no such thing could have been intended by the 1866 Civil Rights Act because "residential segregation was the prevailing pattern almost everywhere in the North," and that the Act was designed to prohibit only "official, community sanctioned discrimination in the South." 392 U.S. at 474–475. Douglas, concurring in the majority opinion, could not resist sniping at Harlan's view: for Douglas it was obvious that all such residential segregation (North *or* South) was precisely the product of the "longstanding and customary pattern" of official racial discrimination premised on the myth of white supremacy that Harlan conceded to be the object of the legislation. 392 U.S. at 449.

Following *Green*, the lower courts generally began to speak and to look at racial identification as an indicia of a continuing dual system. For example, then Circuit Judge Blackmun in *Kemp v. Beasley*, 423 F.2d 851 (8th Cir. 1970), affirmed the secondary school aspect of a desegregation plan because "the two high schools are not racially identifiable . . . [and] the two junior high schools are not racially identifiable." 423 F.2d at 856.[2] "But four [of the dozen or so] elementary schools continue to be racially identifiable and completely black . . . [and,] at the same time, Murmel Heights is a racially identifiable white school." *Id*. All four black schools were constructed in 1959 in black neighborhoods, and by 1970 these four schools served more than one-half of the district's black elementary school children. Blackmun directed that "these five facilities must shed their racial identification." 423 F.2d at 857-858. In "shedding" that racial identification, Blackmun cautioned that racial percentages were but one factor; that some predominantly black and white schools might prove acceptable; and that percentages would probably vary

2. The two high schools were desegregated by pairing; one served grades 11 and 12, the other grade 10. The two junior highs, only 4 blocks apart, were desegregated by voluntary pupil choices. Blackmun, like other judges and courts, offered no suggestion that voluntary methods of pupil assignment had no place in elementary and secondary schooling; he did not assume that compulsory assignments were the norm for public schooling.

year to year due to a number of factors beyond the reach of the Constitution. Blackmun added: "Probably the ultimate answer [concerning racial composition] rests with . . . residential patterns." *Id.*[3]

In *Swann* v. *Charlotte-Mecklenburg Board of Education*, 300 F. Sup. 1358 and 1381, 306 F. Supp. 1299 (W.D.N.C. 1969), District Judge McMillan also focused on the racial identification of the schools and residential segregation. Amplifying Judge Wisdom in *Jefferson County*, he found a causal interaction between school racial identity, construction of black schools in black neighborhoods and white schools in white neighborhoods, residential segregation and customary and officially sanctioned public and private discrimination in housing throughout the metropolitan area: "On the facts in this record and with this background of *de jure* segregation extending the full fifteen years since *Brown I*, this Court is of the opinion that all of the [one-race] schools in the system are illegally segregated." After local school authorities failed to submit any adequate pupil assignment plan, Judge McMillan finally directed that a system-wide desegregation plan be implemented.

On review, a unanimous Supreme Court affirmed 402 U.S. 1 (1971). Although cautioning against "racial balance" as a constitutional requirement (402 U.S. at 16, 24) and warning that at some point no further judicial intervention would be warranted after implementation of a final remedy (even if subsequent demographic changes resegregated the schools, 402 U.S. at 32),[4] the Court approved a system-wide remedy based on Judge McMil-

3. Then Circuit Judge Griffin Bell also read *Green* to focus on "eliminating the racial identification of the schools in a dual system," subject to constraints imposed by residential segregation, *Ellis* v. *Board of Public Instruction*, 423 F.2d 203, 204 (5th Cir. 1979). Bell argued that the neighborhood school—"equidistant zoning"—was the constitutional remedy regardless of the extent of segregation that it might continue in the schools. Any remaining one-race schools would in Bell's view be solely the "result of residential patterns." 465 F.2d at 208. (Following *Swann*, discussed *infra*, Bell dropped his "equidistant zoning"/residential segregation justification for one-race schools and ordered desegregation of all schools.)

4. The Court, however, expressly provided for continuing judicial intervention *after* implementing a remedy upon a showing that "the school authorities or some other agency of the State had deliberately attempted to fix or alter demographic patterns to affect the racial composition of the schools." 402 U.S. at 32. Earlier in the opinion, however, the Court appeared to reserve ruling on whether mere incorporation of such official residential segregation amounts to a constitutional violation. 402 U.S. at 23.

lan's findings concerning the far-reaching effects of the continuing system-wide violation following *Brown*:

> The construction of new schools and the closing of old ones are two of the most important functions of local school authorities and also two of the most complex. They must decide questions of location and capacity in light of population growth, finances, land values, site availability, through an almost endless list of factors to be considered. The result of this will be a decision which, when combined with one technique or another of student assignment will determine the racial composition of the student body in each school in the system. Over the long run, the consequences of the choices will be far reaching. People gravitate toward school facilities, just as schools are located in response to the needs of people. The location of schools may thus influence the pattern of residential development of a metropolitan area and have important impact on composition of inner-city neighborhoods.

402 U.S. at 20.

In addition, although suggesting that some few schools may remain one race in metropolitan areas where minorities are heavily "concentrated in one part of the city" (402 U.S. at 25), the Court nevertheless squarely held:

> in a system with a history of segregation the need for remedial criteria of sufficient specificity to assure a school authority's compliance with its constitutional duty warrants a presumption against schools that are substantially disproportionate in their racial composition. ... The burden on school authorities [that propose the maintenance of such one-race schools in their plans] will be to satisfy the Court that their racial composition is not the result of present or past discriminatory action on their part.

402 U.S. at 26.

The court gave similar shrift to the "neighborhood school"/residential segregation defense for one-race schools:

> Absent a constitutional violation there would be no basis for judicially ordering assignment of students on a racial basis. All things being equal, with no history of discrimination, it might well be desirable to assign pupils to schools nearest their homes. But all things are not equal in a system that has been deliberately constructed and maintained to enforce racial segregation. ...'Racially neutral' assignment plans proposed by school authorities to a district court may be inadequate; such plans may fail to counteract the continuing effects of past school segregation resulting from discriminatory location of

> school sites or distortion of school size in order to achieve or maintain an artificial racial separation. When school authorities prepresent a district court with a 'loaded game board', affirmative action in the form of remedial altering of attendance zones is proper to achieve truly nondiscriminatory assignments. In short, an assignment plan is not acceptable simply because it appears to be neutral.

402 U.S. at 28. Maximum actual desegregation, taking into account the practicalities of the local situation, was the way to dismantle dual systems of elementary and secondary schooling. *Davis* v. *Board of School Comm'rs*, 402 U.S. 33, 37 (1971). The Court at least rejected residential segregation as a defense; only inordinately lengthy bus-rides or racial separation not resulting in any part from the system of Jim Crow caste segregation could justify the perpetuation of dual schooling.

In *Wright* v. *Council of the City of Emporia*, 402 U.S. 451 (1972), Justice Stewart wrote for a 5–4 Court (Burger, Blackmun, Powell, and Rehnquist dissenting on the facts alone.) Although holding that the challenged splintering of the city from the county school system should be judged solely by whether it does or does not hinder the dismantling of the historic countywide dual school system (407 U.S. at 459–460 and 462), Stewart again referred to the principle of caste stigmatization as an aid to his decisional process:

> [W]here an action by school authorities is motivated by a demonstrated discriminatory purpose, the existence of that purpose may add to the discriminatory effect of the action by intensifying the stigma of implied racial inferiority.
> [407 U.S. at 461]

* * * *

> Certainly desegregation is not achieved by splintering a single school system operating "white schools" and "Negro schools" into two systems, each operating unitary schools within its border, where one of the two new systems is, in fact, "white" and the other is, in fact, "Negro." [407 U.S. at 463]

* * * *

> [T]he significance of any racial disparity [here relatively slight] is enhanced [because of the racial identifiability of the schools in terms of quality of facilities, etc.].
>
> [407 U.S. at 465]

* * * *

> The message of this action, coming when it did [two weeks after county-wide, pairing plan ordered], cannot have escaped the Negro children in the County [quoting *Brown*]. [407 U.S. at 406]

In the companion case of *United States* v. *Scotland Neck*, Stewart added for the entire Court:

> The traditional racial identities of the schools in the area would be maintained; the formerly all-white Scotland Neck school would retain a white majority, while the formerly all-Negro Brawley school, a high school located just outside Scotland Neck, would be 91 percent Negro. [407 U.S. at 490]

Stewart argued that whites would respond to "this racial invitation" to move to the identifiably white Scotland Neck schools from the county. Burger, writing for the four *Emporia* dissenters, concurred finding this case dramatically different:

> In a very real sense, the children in this relatively small area would continue to attend "Negro schools" and "white schools" [under the splinter proposal].

407 U.S. at 492.

In *Keyes* v. *School District No. 1*, 413 U.S. 189 (1973), Justice Brennan (Justices Powell and Rehnquist dissenting) applied the stigma or group discrimination principle full force to school authority practices that intentionally segregated a meaningful portion of a school district without benefit of a state compulsory segregation law:

> [W]here plaintiffs prove that the school authorities have carried out a systematic program of segregation affecting a substantial portion of the students, schools, teachers, and facilities within the school system, it is only common sense to conclude that there exists a predicate for a finding of the existence of a dual school system. Several considerations support this conclusion. First, it is obvious that a practice of concentrating Negroes in certain schools by structuring attendance zones or designating "feeder" schools on the basis of race has the reciprocal effect of keeping other nearby schools predominantly white. Similarly, the practice of building a school . . . to a certain size and in a certain location, "with conscious knowledge that it would be a segregated school," 303 F. Supp at 285, has a substantial reciprocal effect on the racial composition of other nearby schools. So also, the use of mobile classrooms, the drafting of student transfer policies, the transportation of students, and the assignment of faculty and staff, on racially identifiable bases, have the

clear effect of earmarking schools according to their racial composition, and this, in turn, together with the elements of student assignment and school construction, may have a profound reciprocal effect on the racial composition of residential neighborhoods within a metropolitan area, thereby causing further racial concentration within the schools. . . . In short, common sense dictates the conclusion that racially inspired school board actions have an impact beyond the particular schools that are the subjects of those actions.

413 U.S. at 200–201.

Justice Brennan continued:

Indeed, to say that a system has a "history of segregation" is merely to say that a pattern of intentional segregation has been established in the past. Thus, be it a statutory dual system or an allegedly unitary system where a meaningful portion of the system is found to be intentionally segregated, the existence of subsequent or other segregated schooling within the same system justifies a rule imposing on the school authorities the burden of proving that this segregated schooling is not also the result of intentionally segregative acts. . . . Intentional school segregation in the past may [also] have been a factor in creating a natural environment for the growth of further segregation.

413 U.S. at 210–213. In such circumstances, the group relief principle applies, and school authorities must desegregate the system of schooling. 413 U.S. at 213–214. Rehnquist objected to the entire thrust of such group discrimination analysis and suggested either (a) limiting the inquiry to individual access only or (b) imposing an insurmountable burden of proof on plaintiffs to show that continuing school segregation resulted solely from the acts of school authorities (and not from residential segregation) as a precondition for any broader actual desegregation relief based on a class violation principle. Powell, in his dissent, took a different tack; he sought to carve a very limiting remedial standard that would ignore the stigma principle altogether: all school segregation would be deemed to violate the constitution because school authorities assign all kids to every school, but the remedy should be an "integrated system" limited to the "neighborhood schools" (with the current levels of residential segregation a justifiable defense).[5]

5. In his subsequent, separate opinion in *Austin, Independent School District* v. *United States*, 429 U.S. 990 (1976), Powell removed the gloves from his conundrum of all violation/no remedy: Powell argued that residential segregation is

In *Milliken* v. *Bradley*, 418 U.S. 717 (1974) (Milliken I), the cross-district case, Chief Justice Burger, writing for a 5–4 Court, avoided all consideration of the stigma/group discrimination principle because of the way he stated the case—i.e., no allegations in the complaint (true), and thus no proof nor findings (false) of anything but Detroit-only effects resulting from Detroit-only violations:

> The record before us, voluminous as it is, contains evidence of *de jure* segregated conditions only in the Detroit schools. . . . *Brown*, *Green*, *Swann*, *Scotland Neck*, and *Emporia*, each addressed the issue of constitutional wrong in terms of an established geographic and administrative school system populated by both Negro and white children. In such a context, terms such as "unitary" and "dual" system, and "racially identifiable schools," have meaning, and the necessary federal authority to remedy the constitutional wrong is firmly established. But the remedy is necessarily designed, as all remedies are, to restore the victims of discriminatory conduct to the position they would have occupied in the absence of such conduct. Disparate treatment of white and Negro students occurred within the Detroit school system, and not elsewhere, and on this record the remedy must be limited to that system. The view of the dissenters, that the existence of a dual system in *Detroit* can be made the basis for a decree requiring cross-district transportation of pupils cannot be supported on the grounds that it represents merely the devising of a suitably flexible remedy for the violation of rights already established by our prior decisions. It can be supported only by drastic expansion of the constitutional right itself, an expansion without any support in either constitutional principle or precedent.

418 U.S. at 745–746.

By cabining the inquiry from the outset within the geographic limits of the Detroit School District, Burger avoided full consideration of the application of the stigma principle to racial ghettoization of blacks within the core city of the metropolitan area, while giving lipservice to the property of inter-district relief

the primary cause of school segregation; and there can be no violation if school authorities merely "neutrally" incorporate rather than exacerbate this segregation in their racially neutral student assignment policies. Powell's shifting positions on "violation" appear to be a "no busing result" searching for 5 votes; but his decisional rationale is based on limiting the understanding of any wrong to denial of *individual* access (to homes and schools), to restrictions on individual "choice" and "institutional diversity," rather than class discrimination stigmatizing blacks as a group as second-class citizens. See also *Regents of University of California* v. *Bakke*, 438 U.S. 265, 295-299, 311-315 (1978).

in the "appropriate" case where inter-district segregative effects have been pleaded, proven, and found. 418 U.S. at 744–745.

Justice Stewart, concurring separately, seemed to go somewhat further. He conceded that proof of *public* contribution to segregation of blacks in the inner-city surrounded by whites in an exclusionary ring would provide a basis for inter-district desegregation; but he argued that:

> In this case, however, no such inter-district violation was shown. Indeed, no evidence at all concerning the administration of schools outside the city of Detroit was presented other than the fact that these schools contained a higher proportion of white pupils than did the schools within the city. Since the mere fact of different racial compositions in contiguous districts does not itself imply or constitute a violation of the Equal Protection Clause in the absence of a showing that such disparity was imposed, fostered, or encouraged by the State or its political subdivisions, it follows that no inter-district violation was shown in this case.

In an accompanying footnote, Stewart added:

> "... segregative acts within the city alone cannot be presumed to have produced—and no factual showing was made that they did produce—an increase in the number of Negro students *in the city as a whole.* It is this essential fact of a predominantly Negro school population in Detroit—caused by *unknown and perhaps unknowable* factors such as in-migration, birth rates, economic changes, or cumulative acts of private racial fears—that accounts for the "growing core of Negro schools," a "core" that has grown to include virtually the entire city. The Constitution simply does not allow federal courts to attempt to change that situation unless and until it is shown that the State, or its political subdivisions, have contributed to cause the situation to exist. No record has been made in this case showing that the racial composition of the Detroit school population or that residential patterns within Detroit and in the surrounding areas were in any significant measure caused by governmental activity.

418 U.S. at 755–756 and n.2. Stewart's reasoning saves the stigma principle by finding its invocation *unwarranted* by the record evidence in *this case.* Yet it represents a startling turnabout from Stewart's view in *Jones* v. *Mayer* of the caste nature and discriminatory causes of racial ghettoization in metropolitan America.

Marshall's dissent (along with those of White and Douglas) argue that Stewart's view of the record evidence is blind; and they stress the continuing relevance of the stigma principle even when confronting a local governmental boundary line. The 14th Amendment, in their view, does speak expressly in terms of the State; and the Reconstruction Amendments speak to a customary caste system of public and private action that was never neatly confined within the boundaries of local governmental units, let alone government itself.

Dayton Board of Education v. *Brinkman* (Dayton I), 433 U.S. 406 (1977), also sought to limit the stigma or group discrimination principle in applying the constitutional standard of purposeful discrimination to limited violation "findings" of the trial court (which were not "reversed" nor expressly "supplemented" by the Court of Appeals). Justice Rehnquist, thereby restricted any remedy to the "isolated instances" of violation, i.e., optional zones affecting only three high schools, whose effects, "manifestly," were not systemwide. This view allowed the Supreme Court to leave review of the extensive violation record to the lower courts under a standard of causation suitable for confining any continuing effects of any violations to the maximum extent feasible: any desegregation remedy would be limited to the "incremental segregative effect" specifically resulting from particular constitutional violations. 433 U.S. at 420.

On the same day, however, a unanimous Supreme Court also affirmed the provisions of sweeping "ancillary relief" and "educational components" in the second Detroit school case for the presumed harm resulting to black school children as a group from a long history of intentional segregation. Unlike the decision in *Dayton I*, the Court accepted unproven causal connections between past wrong and current educational harm. See *Milliken* v. *Bradley*, 433 U.S. 267, 282–283, 287–288 (1977) (Milliken II). It seemed that the Court might be saying that the full implications of the group discrimination principle would be ignored if the remedy were perceived as too unsettling (e.g. "busing"), but credited in other instances if the remedy were perceived as more generally acceptable and beneficial (e.g. improved education for the "victims" of the violation).

In both *Columbus Board of Education* v. *Penick* and *Dayton II*, however, the Sixth Circuit concluded that, although Ohio law since 1888 had ostensibly forbidden the operation of separate public schools for black and white children, Columbus and Dayton school authorities, through official administrative policy, action and default had accomplished the same result as the "southern" segregation laws: a system of racially dual schooling. Accordingly, the Sixth Circuit held that an across-the-board desegregation remedy was essential to the elimination of all vestiges of state-imposed segregation. Many observers predicted that the Supreme Court would take this opportunity to continue to limit the group relief/class discrimination principle, at least for urban school desegregation cases where residential segregation and busing affect the feasibility of any possible wide-ranging desegregation remedy. In 5–4 majority opinions written by Justice White (joined by Justices Brennan, Marshall, Blackmun, and Stevens), however, the Supreme Court affirmed the Sixth Circuit in *Dayton II*, 433 U.S. 526 (1979), and *Columbus*, 443 U.S. 449 (1979). Limiting *Dayton I*'s restrictive rationale to more limited violation findings, the Court agreed with the Sixth Circuit that:

- The local boards had intentionally segregated a substantial portion of the black (and white) students at the time of *Brown*, resulting in a basically dual system of schooling. 443 U.S. at 456–8 and 443 U.S. at 534–7.
- After *Brown*, the local boards not only failed to disestablish this dual system but also perpetuated and exacerbated the dual system through the time of trial. 443 U.S. 461–3 and 443 U.S. at 539–40.
- Once plaintiffs prove intentional segregation affecting a substantial portion of the system, defendant school authorities bear the burden of showing that other and subsequent segregation in the system is unrelated, not caused by the intentional segregation, and not affected by segregative intent. 443 U.S. 458–462, 467–468 and 443 U.S. at 537–9, 541–2.
- With respect to the causal interaction between schools and housing, the Court noted that the evidence confirmed that intentional school segregation is a contributing cause of housing segregation. 443 U.S. at 465 n. 13.
- The affirmative evidence of a system of dual schooling at the time of *Brown*, post-*Brown* failures to dismantle, and post-*Brown* systematic perpetuation of a dual system justified the Sixth Circuit's determination "to trace the current, system-wide segregation back to the purposefully dual system of the 1950s and to subsequent acts of intentional discrimination." 443 U.S. at 541; also 443 U.S. at 463–465.

In sum, the Court in *Columbus* and *Dayton II* reaffirmed the primary principles of *Green*, *Swann*, *Wright*, and *Keyes*: intentional school segregation has wide-ranging and long-lasting consequences and caste implications that can only be remedied by actual desegregation; and once a systematic program of segregation has been uncovered, school authorities bear the responsibility either to eradicate the full impact of their discriminatory conduct or to show what current segregation, if any, cannot be traced to coninuing or prior racial discrimination. This affirmation of the primary products of the racial identification/stigma principle was complete but narrow.[6]

In addition to implementing the twin principles of affirmative desegregation and broad ancillary relief from group segregation in elementary and secondary schools, federal courts are also with increasing resolve prohibiting school authorities from implementing plans that would disproportionately burden identifiably black as compared to white interests. Thus, courts have rejected plans that would require "one-way" desegregation, disproportionately close black schools, disproportionately bus black students, or resegregate black students within schools in separate classes or tracks, and the like. *See, e.g., Evans* v. *Buchanan*, 447 F. Supp. 982 (D. Del. 1978), aff'd 582 F.2d 750 (3rd Cir. 1978). In short, the courts have concluded that free access for individual blacks to historically white elementary or secondary schools is insufficient to remedy the *system* of group segregation by which the white majority seeks to ghettoize blacks into a separate caste and stigmatize the class of blacks as inherently inferior or undeserving. Decision on this issue was slow in coming and has recently been subject to increasing challenge from within and without the Supreme Court. By the narrowest of margins, resi-

6. Justice Stewart (joined by Chief Justice Burger) concurred in the judgment of the Court in *Columbus* on the grounds that the evidence as found by the district court (a) supported its finding of intentionally segregative conduct causing current segregation in a meaningful portion of the school district and (b) properly shifted the burden of proof to school authorities to justify the remaining segregation as adventitious, which they failed to do. 443 U.S. at 475–9. Justice Stewart (joined by Chief Justice Burger) dissented in *Dayton II* on the grounds (a) that he would accept the trials courts quite different findings that virtually no intentional discrimination was practiced after 1954 and (b) that he did not agree that any shifting in the burden of proof from plaintiffs to defendants was warranted upon a showing that the Board operated a basically dual system in 1954. 443 U.S. at 470–5. Justice Powell, dissenting in both cases, argued for an access principle on the ground that school segregation resulted from demographic and family choices over which school boards had no control and which the Court ought not condemn. 443 U.S. at 487–489. Justice Rehnquist, dissenting in both cases, restated his strict view of causation and challenged the Court's class discrimination/group relief premise as articulated in *Keyes*, *Swann*, and *Green*. 443 U.S. at 495–525.

dential segregation is still rejected as a defense to continued one-race schooling, while local school district boundaries have served to limit but not immunize judicial scrutiny of the extent of segregation. Finally, free choice as a method of pupil assignment has been rejected only where it proves inadequate to desegregate a formerly intentionally segregated system. As a result, the law of this land for elementary and secondary schools is that group discrimination against blacks as a class (as well as denial to individuals of meaningful access to particular schools) is prohibited by the Constitution.

Post-*Brown* Desegregation Standards

The tension between theories of group relief and individual access has not been resolved for higher education. The Supreme Court has yet to speak on the subject, some 27 years after *Brown*, even though the "all deliberate speed" standard has long since been jettisoned.

There are fewer lower Court decisions; and none provide any clear guidance on this fundamental issue. The tribulations and travail of Autherine Lucy and James Meredith in securing access to the University of Alabama and the University of Mississippi provide eloquent testimony to the difficulty for many years of opening whites-only institutions to *any* black person that aspires to higher education. To this day there is also suspicion that the increasing reliance on standardized test for admission during the decades when blacks sought to tear down barriers to formerly whites-only colleges, universities and graduate schools was premised, in part, on their effectiveness in excluding most blacks or limiting their admission to black colleges with lower cut-off scores. Absent evidentiary proof that such tests racially discriminate against black applicants, however, the access principle promises no relief (beyond affirmative recruiting of the "talented tenth") for increasing the number of blacks at historically white institutions of higher education. Under *Bakke*, 438 U.S. 265, there is even some doubt as to the manner and extent to which any State may seek voluntarily to increase the "diversity" of its traditionally white schools by acting affirmatively to *admit* blacks with lower SAT scores. Nor does the access principle require States that formerly mandated Jim Crow segregation to upgrade the institutional mission, facilities, faculties, teaching, and job placement connections of the traditionally black schools that for decades were funded and administered by the dominant white majority to train blacks only for second-class status. Under the access principle, however, historic deprivation of black institutions compared to white may be ignored so long as they are *now* funded on some race-neutral principle and are now open to all comers meeting non-racial admission and hiring standards of the particular school. The marketplace for students and faculty, voluntarism, and the State's determination of how best to provide for higher education will then control. Under the access standard, black students aspiring to higher education and black colleges seeking continued or increased support must look to the political process for any larger redress.

Yet, the access standard has particular appeal because higher education is not compelled, choice of school is ultimately made by individual matriculation, and academic freedom adds legitimacy to claims for institutional autonomy. It also allows the States to make whatever plans for expansion or contraction of traditional white and black institutions and for creation of new facilities that they may wish, while avoiding difficult questions concerning any continuing inequities and barriers, racial identifications and channeling, and public support of individual choices based on race resulting from the historic Jim Crow systems of higher education. All of these factors may play some part in decisions such as *A.S.T.A.* v. *Alabama Public School and College Authority*, 289 F. Supp. 784, 789 (M.D. Ala. 1968), aff'd mem., 393 U.S. 400 (1969), that adopt race-neutral access as the guiding constitutional principle. Coupled with a State's voluntary promise to support the historically black colleges at some modestly enhanced levels of per pupil funding, faculty training and program offering, the access principle becomes very attractive to States who want the least disruption of higher education, to blacks who want to save black schools, and to courts looking for a principled way out of a potentially divisive issue, particularly where the effectiveness of more sweeping class remedies and group relief is largely untried and open to serious question. The recent settlements in North Carolina and Louisiana evidence the political attractiveness of such a result.

In addition, Justice Powell has rejected the underpinning for any group discrimination theory in *Bakke*. He labels such "stigma" analysis a "subjective judgment that is standardless." 438 U.S. at 294 n. 34. He argues for individual access and institutional diversity and autonomy for higher education on the premise that the Fourteenth Amendment protects blacks no more than the many diverse "ethnic minorities" that make the nation "a majority of minorities." 438 U.S. at 292–9. Although reserving judgment on the propriety of limited class relief in a case with "particularized findings of past discrimination," 438 U.S. at 307–9, Powell appears ready to opt for an access principle for higher education.

On the other hand, some lower courts have relied on *Green*'s principles of group discrimination, caste stigmatization, continuing racial identification, and class relief in evaluating the propriety of continuing or expanding arguably duplicative white institutions near historic black institutions. See *Norris* v. *State Council of Higher Education*, 327 F.Supp 1368, 1737 (E.D. Va. 1971); *Geier* v. *University of Tennessee*, 427 F.Supp 644 (M.D. Tenn. 1977), aff'd 597 F.2d 1056, 1065–1066 (1979). In addition, courts have begun to express their reservations about any remedial plan that (1) fails to take into account the special problems of minority students through appropriate ancillary relief (e.g. financial aid, recruiting, tutoring, etc.), (2) seeks to place a greater burden of desegregation on black schools or black students than white, or (3) fails to come to grips with the entire state *system* of dual schooling for higher education. See, e.g., *Adams* v. *Richardson*, 480 F.2d 1159, 1164 (D.C. Cir. 1973); *Adams* v. *Califano*, 430 F. Supp. 117, 120 (D.D. 1977). Finally in *Bakke*, Justices Brennan, White, Marshall, and Blackmun credit the stigmatizing nature of caste discrimination as the fundamental group wrong that must be fully redressed. 438 U.S. at 357–362.

Yet *none* of these cases comes to grips with how the class discrimination and group relief principle should be applied in the particular circumstances of higher education to dismantle an historically dual system throughout a particular State.[7] Nevertheless certain requirements are self-evident from the nature of the

7. The lack of judicial standards is a result, in part, of the attempt to resolve the issue administratively under Title VI through OCR administrative proceedings rather than through trials and equitable decrees in federal courts, with review by the Supreme Court. OCR's revised criteria, however, cannot be viewed as the likely final word until reviewed by the judiciary because of the Supreme Court's apparent determination that Title VI provides no more protection for blacks and other minorities than the Fourteenth Amendment. See *University of California Board of Regents* v. *Bakke*, 438 U.S. 265, 284 (Powell), 328 (Brennan, White, Marshall, Blackmun).

principle. The wholesale closing of black colleges could *not* be permitted by any equity court; nor would jurisdiction be relinquished by any court until the plan *worked* to remove, insofar as feasible, all objective and intangible vestiges of a system that deemed blacks inferior and suited for training as second-class citizens, while subsidizing the opportunity for whites to gain the full range and benefits of higher education. Beyond that, the state-wide nature of higher education would permit considerably more imaginative and far-reaching remedies than heretofore contemplated for elementary and secondary education. Unlike elementary and secondary desegregation, local school district boundaries and residential segregation provide *no* basis for justifying continuing segregation in higher education. In addition, the necessity for plans which lead to students matriculating to colleges and universities on a voluntary basis compels consideration of wider ranging remedies than mandatory pupil reassignments. As a result, purported "mergers" or elimination of program duplication of nearby black and white institutions may be doomed to failure if students continue to make application and matriculation decisions based on racial stereotypes and the legacy of Jim Crow practices of separate and unequal higher education.

If the group relief principle is to be implemented, then there is a critical need to consider what substantial enhancement and program "magnets" are needed to make traditionally black colleges generally perceived as unique, first-class components a single state system of higher education rather than "second class" vocational centers for "inherently inferior blacks" under Jim Crow segregation. At the same time, incentives for students attending historically opposite-race schools and incentives for institutions enrolling students from their historic minority race must be tried. Similarly, insofar as remediation or other special access and learning programs are required as an ancillary measure to insure that blacks are not disproportionately excluded from higher education during the dismantling process, consideration must be given to operating such programs on an integrated basis in traditionally white, as well as black, schools.

If the goal is to dismantle state-wide dual systems of higher education in order to remedy caste segregation of blacks as a group from whites, then the remedies to be considered must include fundamental restructuring, albeit *within* the context of voluntary student choices and the legitimate purposes of college and graduate training. The novelty of such thinking about fundamental restructuring, however, may so put off hide-bound and harried educators and courts wary of the limits of judicial review that the access principle will gain increasing support at the expense of the class discrimination/caste stigmatization/group relief principle.

Conclusion

Given the historic context, political interests, and the lack of clear judicial guidelines, it is understandable why the debate and decisions concerning "desegregation" of colleges and universities seek to "balance" constituencies and to "compromise" policy concerns rather than apply generally applicable constitutional principles, imaginatively and sensitively, to the particular circumstances of higher education in each State. Without investigating the available proof and particular circumstances of any State, however, my litigation instinct suggests: (a) that the current racial identification of most colleges and universities can be traced in substantial part *and* significant detail to the continuing effects of dual schooling pre-*Brown* and to the perpetuation of the basic racial division post-*Brown*; and (b) that the voluntary nature of student application and matriculation and faculty decisions in higher education does not necessarily limit constitutional analyses to the individual access rather than the group discrimination principle. In my opinion, therefore, the various interested parties should be actively considering the merits and potential of much more wide-ranging and novel class relief to overcome the vestiges of continuing dual systems of higher education. That is the only way that negotiated settlements between State and federal executive officials will (a) survive any meaningful judicial review and (b) provide meaningful relief from one fundamental aspect of the wrong of Jim Crow segregation.

In an area where residential segregation, busing, and local district boundaries do not make dismantling dual systems difficult, providing complete group relief from discriminatory systems of higher education hardly seems an insurmountable problem. But no one seems to have offered much creative thinking about remedies that might actually desegregate; only band-aids and the hope that time will provide some attrition of some perceived problem (or relief from some pressure to desegregate) are the "solutions" that have been tried or suggested. Whether bolder initiatives will be planned and brought forward depends on events, commitments, and resources that must be the subject of another's ruminations. But the point is that the principle of group relief from historic caste segregation should apply to former dual systems of higher education. As a result, "desegregation" of higher education means more than "open access" or another means of preserving historic white universities as "white" and historic black colleges as "black". Unless politics leads to limitation of the constitutional objective, the State's duty is to come forward with a plan that realistically promises to integrate the State system of dual schooling in higher education on a nondiscriminatory basis.

5 Toward Desegregation and Enhancement

Albert H. Berrian

Enhancement of historically black public institutions of higher education—of a kind that will enable them to be responsive to the social, cultural, knowledge, research, public service and extension needs of higher education users within the institutions' service areas—is a relatively new phenomenon. It grows, in large part, out of the higher education desegregation process, which began after the historic 1954 Supreme Court decision and gained momentum after 1969. Between 1963 and 1970 federal courts conducted an extensive review of the Department of Health, Education and Welfare's (HEW's) efforts to adopt measures that would overcome the effects of past segregation on their higher education systems. Following the finding that efforts in states where dual systems of education had been maintained were inadequate, the United States District Court for the District of Columbia, under the urging of the Legal Defense Fund, ordered six states to submit new desegregation plans and to set specific standards for the plans.[1] This action triggered the making of specific commitments, which included consideration of enhanced roles of historically black institutions.

Criteria, certain aspects of which are currently under question, were issued to assist states to comply with constitutional standards as these are reflected in the 14th Amendment of the constitution and provisions of Title VI of the Civil Rights Act of 1964. Voluntary compliance was hoped for. Failure of such compliance was followed by federal pressure through administrative and court means. This kind of pressure is now giving away to increasingly cooperative behavior among parties with conflicting

1. These states included Arkansas, Florida, Georgia, North Carolina, Oklahoma and Virginia.

interests and a desire to keep the nation's best interests in the forefront of their thinking. Your speaker, in fact, is here as the representative of an organization which has for fifteen years urged rational approaches to the problem of desegregation and the enhancement of all viable struggling institutions, whether historically white or black.

The time of this meeting represents a point where even the most inimical of parties are concluding good faith negotiations that "promise realistically and promptly to eliminate all vestiges of dual systems of higher education." Fortunately, the federal government has proceeded out of a conviction that the states themselves must be the principal architects of the newly emerging desegregation plans. This approach seems reasonable, since the questions that have to be addressed when enhancement is the issue (those of academic programs, physical facilities, available resources, etc.) represent areas uniquely within the expertise of authorities charged with day-to-day institutional operational responsibilities.

It is reassuring to have organizations such as the American Council on Education and Aspen Institute for Humanistic Studies take an active role in facilitating a politico-social process that has too long been left to the courts. The dangers in doing so prematurely are well understood, but it is encouraging to know that distinguished educational organizations are no longer content with allowing courts to be the only principal actors on the side of carrying out affirmative responsibilities.

Measures deemed necessary to ensure higher education desegregation have included student recruitment, enrollment, academic and financial support systems, other-race grants, interinstitutional cooperation, governing bodies and administrative staff and faculties. Special emphasis has, however, been placed on the development, within the historically black institutions, of high yield and higher level programs and the improvement of their physical plants and general environments. Your speaker's emphasis will be on the programmatic enhancement of the historically black institutions, for this is the most critical of areas, if these institutions are to survive and be of use to the total public.

Use of all institutions by the public is a matter of major concern in this very state where our seminar is being hosted. The lead editorial in the September 3rd edition of the "Baltimore

Sun" decried the fact that the state's black colleges were being allowed to lag, that as a consequence poor students were being denied the opportunity for a high-quality hometown university education, and that the Governor and General Assembly were bound to "unify Maryland education on a rational, regional basis as the only hope for preserving and strengthening Maryland's black colleges and developing a prestigious higher education system for the state as a whole."

One does not intend to dwell on the Maryland situation, except to say that it has been, until very recently, generalizable. Other states have, through the submission of acceptable Desegregation Plans and Consent Decrees, made more progress than Maryland. Morgan State University, for example, an historically black public institution with a statewide urban mission, does not even have a downtown presence, let alone an outreach program that can allow it to service the heavy influx of black and Hispanic urban dwellers into Montgomery and Prince George counties. Neither has the continued downtown growth of the University of Baltimore and the obvious overlap in function between these two state-supported urban institutions been appropriately addressed. One must conclude that for such a situation to exist, political and racial factors have been and still are allowed to outweigh the need for sound, cooperative educational planning under responsible leadership and coordination.

We must and should move on, for our discussion has much wider implications. An overview of the capability gap in the nation's historically black public institutions should serve to provide a framework within which to consider their programmatic development.

An Overview

No HBI, with the near exception of Howard University (a private sector institution, enjoying federal support), has a comprehensive research and development capability. None are viewed by the State Department as serious candidates for delivering development services to third world nations. Few are engaged in the delivery of public or extension services on anything resembling a major scale. Only three—none public—can deliver allied health services of any consequences or train allied health professionals. Indeed, no public HBI is equipped to supply professionals with terminal or near-terminal training, except within the field of education, and even here the capacity to train psychometricians and system-oriented persons is limited.

If they had been treated fairly, what kind of professionals would at least some of the HBIs been able to produce? Physicians, osteopaths, dentists, nurse practitioners, a comprehensive array of allied health workers, veterinarians, clinical psychologist psychometricians, life scientists, optometrists, chemical and petroleum engineers, geologists, mining engineers, aerospace engineers, metallurgists, system analysts, and others.

Until the late 1960's the historically black institutions represented virtually the only avenue open to blacks into the university and the professions. This situation has now changed, with only 20 percent of blacks in the historically black institutions, but as it is often pointed out by the National Association for Equal Opportunity (NAFEO) and the National Advisory Committee on Black Higher Education and Black Colleges and Universities, a disproportionately high percentage of baccalaureate degrees is still produced through these institutions. The same would be true of graduate and professional school degrees, were these institutions in a position to grant them. As matters stand, graduate and professional school enrollment is declining nationally, with black enrollment down 8 percent against 6 percent for white enrollment. More ground is, therefore, being lost, during a period of general retrenchment—a loss which blacks and the nation can ill-afford. Even if one were to make the case that there is a surplus of professionals in some areas, no areas except perhaps education and the applied social sciences can point to a surplus of blacks (or Hispanics or American Indians).

An understanding of the breadth and depth of the problem is aided by a statistical view of it. The tables below were prepared by the Mississippi Commission on Higher Education to illustrate the percentage of Ph.D's held by minorities nationally:

There are gaps in the table. It is not shown, for example, that there are only 6,000 or so black M.D.'s out of a national total approaching 400,000 or 2,000 dentists out of a total of 120,000 or more. Neither does it show that this situation stands little chance of correction, with 4,000 current black medical school enrollees out of 60,000 or 1,000 black dental school enrollees out of 20,000. There is no mystery about any of this, since no historically black public institution has ever received a medical or dental school, and there are only two full-blown medical and dental schools in

TABLE 1

PERCENTAGE OF Ph.D's HELD BY MINORITIES—NATIONAL

Department	Black	Hispanic	Asian	American Indian	Minority Total
Agriculture & Home Economics					
Agriculture & Biological Engineering	—	—	7.4	.7	8.10
Agricultural Economics	1.6	1.1	3.8	.7	7.20
Agricultural & Extension Education	12.6	1.1	2.1	2.1	17.90
Agricultural & Experimental Statistics	.8	.8	7.2	0	8.80
Agronomy	2.1	1.5	3.3	.3	7.20
Animal Science	1.1	1.1	5.4	.9	8.50
Biochemistry	1.5	1.0	6.8	.5	9.80
Dairy Science	1.1	1.1	5.4	.9	8.50
Entomology	1.5	1.1	2.5	.2	5.30
Home Economics	3.2	—	2.1	1.1	6.40
Horticulture	3.4	.7	4.0	—	8.10
Landscape Architecture	3.2	1.6	.8	0	5.60
Plant Pathology	.8	.4	6.0	1.1	8.30
Poultry Science	1.1	1.1	5.4	.9	8.50
Architecture					
Architecture	1.0	—	—	.3	1.30
Arts & Sciences					
Anthropology	1.9	1.1	1.1	.7	4.80
Art	2.9	1.5	1.1	.4	5.90
Biological Sciences	1.7	.9	4.1	.4	7.10
Chemistry	1.4	.75	7.3	.23	9.68
Communication	2.7	.6	.6	.4	4.30
Computer Science/ Statistics	.9	1.8	5.4	—	8.10
English	1.7	.5	1.1	.6	3.90
Foreign Languages	1.6	5.3	1.2	.2	8.30
Geology & Geography	1.9	.2	1.5	.9	4.50
History	1.9	1.0	1.4	.5	4.80
Mathematics	1.0	.7	5.4	.4	7.50
Philosophy & Religion	1.9	.4	3.8	.3	6.40
Physics	.67	.7	6.0	.23	7.60
Political Science	2.7	1.3	2.6	.2	6.80
Psychology	2.4	.9	.9	.5	4.70
Social Work	11.4	3.4	2.3	.4	17.50
Sociology	4.1	1.0	1.9	.3	7.30

Business & Industry					
Accounting	3.6	—	5.5	—	9.10
Business Statistics & Data Processing	4.0	4.0	8.0	—	16.00
Economics	1.1	.7	2.9	.43	5.13
Finance	5.0	2.5	2.5	—	10.00
Management					
Marketing	4.0	2.0	4.0	2.0	12.00
Education					
Adult Education	6.8	1.8	1.1	.6	10.30
Educational Administration & Community College Education	10.8	1.9	.6	.73	14.03
Educational Psychology	4.2	.8	1.5	.9	7.40
Elementary, Secondary & Special Education	8.9	1.7	.8	.6	12.00
Health Education, Physical Education & Recreation	2.7	.5	.7	.4	4.30
Industrial & Occupational Education	6.1	.5	.5	.6	7.70
Music Education	5.1	.2	1.2	.2	6.70
Student Personnel & Counselor Education	7.1	1.3	.4	.6	9.40
Engineering					
Aerospace Engineering	.4	.4	7.3	.7	8.80
Chemical Engineering	.4	1.3	16.3	.2	18.20
Civil Engineering	.7	.4	17.0	.5	18.60
Electrical Engineering	1.2	.4	11.6	.1	13.30
Engineering Graphics	NA	NA	NA	NA	NA
Industrial Engineering	1.1	.4	4.2	—	5.70
Mechanical Engineering	1.2	.4	13.2	.2	15.00
Nuclear Engineering	.6	.6	7.5	—	8.70
Petroleum Engineering	NA	NA	NA	NA	NA
Forest Resources					
Forestry	0.0	0.0	2.2	0.0	2.20
Wildlife & Fisheries	0.5	0.0	3.6	0.5	4.60
Food Science & Technology	NA	NA	NA	NA	NA
Veterinary Medicine					
Veterinary Medicine	1.1	1.1	4.4	—	6.60

the private historically black sector. The only veterinary school is in the private sector (at Tuskegee Institute); of the three pharmacy schools, one is in the private sector. Of the 2,573 engineering doctorates earned in 1977–78, only 15 were earned by blacks, against 25 by Hispanics and 1,874 by foreign nationals. Five of the degrees were actually in computer related fields; 15 engineering specialities were totally unrepresented.[2] No black doctorates came out in electrical or mechanical engineering, the specialties in which the highest number of engineering doctorates is produced.

At the master degree level, a level now reached in engineering by two private and two public black institutions, only 199 blacks graduated in 1977–78, against 239 Hispanics, 784 Asians and 3,579 foreign nationals. Equal numbers came out (54) in electrical and electronic engineering and in civil engineering. Mechanical and general engineering also appear to be areas in which some breakthrough might be expected at this level. Nine came out in marine engineering at the masters level, but three or less in aerospace, agricultural, architectual, bio-medical, ceramic, mechanical, environmental, general, metallurgical, mining and petroleum engineering and operations research. The importance of these specialties for technological advancement, areas in which the nation's historically black land-grant institutions and Howard, Tuskegee, Hampton and the University of the District of Columbia need upgrading, is abundantly clear.

The life sciences can be subjected to a similar analysis. Only three private institutions, Howard, Meharry and Atlanta University (to a very limited degree) are capable of producing life scientists with the highest level training. Private sector historically black institutions have had to assume a massive burden, simply to keep blacks from near total exclusion from gaining experiences in scientific research of a bio-chemical and botanical nature. Until recently, four private institutions, Howard, Meharry, Atlanta University and Tuskegee Institute, have borne the brunt of this burden.

One can dwell on past inequities and lost opportunities, but this will lead nowhere. In fact, it might prove to be counter productive. The question is one of beginning where we are and working through massive total citizen involvement to effect the

2. See Table 7 in the 1979 NASULGC, publication, *Supply and Demand of Scientists and Engineers in Energy Related Areas.* Also see Addendum I.

equalization of institutional and individual opportunities. We know, of course, that there are barriers to black student performance in certain areas, even if increased programmatic opportunities were to exist. The majority of minority students from the lower socio-economic circumstances (and data indicate that 90% came from these circumstances) have been underserved by the elementary and secondary schools system. Most have not had the benefit of college preparatory training, and so perform below the national average on college-entry achievement tests.[3] This means that there are deficits in their verbal and quantitative skills which need to be addressed before the student can benefit from post-secondary education in certain areas. Verbal skills need to be raised in order to guarantee success in most subjects. Candidates for life sciences and medical and engineering careers are expected to have had a background in one or more sciences and in mathematics up to and preferably including calculus. Only a monitored, integrated approach to developmental education, based upon minimum exit standards, will make opportunities to enter the worlds of the science and engineering professionals realizable.

Historically white mainline institutions servicing large numbers of socio-economically disadvantaged students, as well as historically black institutions, must implement viable developmental education programs, if they are realistically to promote equality of professional access.

Cooperative Planning

The application of sophisticated cooperative planning techniques over reasonable time spans represents the most logical approach to working our way out of an American dilemma. This approach does, however, require enlightened leadership and a workforce made up of persons of goodwill. Higher education institutions belong to the public and with the exception of those of an international or national character, they belong to the surrounding public(s). Institutions with international reputations, of which Harvard and Howard Universities are prime examples, might thrive without a sense of ownership on the part of the local citizenry. To a much lesser extent, this might be true of institutions of national character, such as Rensselaer Polytechnic Institute and Morehouse College. Some institutions have a

3. See Addendum II.

statewide character—Louisiana Tech, for example—and when a dual system of higher education existed so did practically all of the black public institutions. This is changing rapidly, as state flagship institutions begin to share major teaching and research responsibilities, and as higher education desegregation plans result in the intensified recruitment, on the part of the historically white institutions, of black students.[4] Kentucky represents a case in point. Only 14 percent of the state's black students attend Kentucky State University, when formerly practically all of them did so.

During the summer, your speaker joined the Kentucky State University president, the chairman of the Chamber of Commerce and a state legislator on a local television program. The purpose was to review the history of Kentucky State University, to announce the programs and services scheduled for its future, and to acquaint local citizens with the fact that the university had the full endorsement of well-respected community and state leaders. It was expected that the one-hour television program, along with other public relations efforts, would enhance the image of the university and make it more attractive for the local citizenry and re-validate the university for traditional clients who now go elsewhere so as to have access to wider educational options. It was clearly understood by everyone involved in the taping that for Kentucky State University to survive and be placed in a position to offer the kind and level of programs, public services and continuing education services required by persons living and working in the state capital, that local *psychological acceptance* of the institution would be required.

Local acceptance will establish a base for state acceptance, and the meeting of institutional resource requirements is based upon increased local demand for services. In the past, and under dual systems, that would not have been the case. The state would have established a parallel institution, as was done in New Orleans a generation ago and in Nashville less than a generation ago. Unless the new federal administration abdicates its legal responsibilities for reasons of socio-political expediency, this old course of action will no longer be possible and historically black institutions enabled, as partners in unitary state systems, to meet

4. In North Carolina, for example, the State University at Raleigh and East Carolina are beginning to share this responsibility, with the University of North Carolina at Charlotte standing in the wings.

needs based upon general demand and available resources. These institutions must, however, belong to all of the people, although they may continue to meet the special needs of black citizens for as long as such special needs are identifiable.

Training opportunities for blacks and other minorities have been enhanced through an opening up of the American higher education system. Fully 80 percent of all black college students, as mentioned earlier, are in so-called, mainstream institutions. Despite the fact that attrition is high, there is increasing evidence that systems approaches to developmental education are beginning to reduce attrition. Training opportunities for blacks in historically black institutions, which boasted of providing the only sympathetic learning environments to blacks have not kept pace with those in mainstream institutions. Organized planning inputs from the environments of these institutions are the only answer to their survival and further development.

In this regard, educational users must be identified, their needs and interests assessed and the gaps between needs and interests and existing programs and services pinpointed. This can be done by a consulting firm. With information about user needs and interests, existing program facilities and resources, user representatives can be brought together as a potential steering committee for input into the historically black institutions' planning processes. Input, as described, is expected to uncover new human, physical and financial resources.

One does not wish here to deemphasize the importance of the federal government as a catalyst for the initiation of state and local enhancement efforts. The federal role has borne fruit in the form of recently signed consent decrees in North Carolina, South Carolina and Louisiana and in continuing negotiations in southern and border states. Indeed, the legal conditions for making cooperative planning at local levels workable, are relatively ideal. In point of fact, a close examination of what happened in South Carolina and Louisiana will reveal a greater degree of voluntarism than one would suspect.

There are untapped federal involvement possibilities that would not infringe on state and local duties and responsibilities. Historically black institutions could be mobilized to undertake training responsibilities in science, engineering and management areas, in view of the national economic consequence of a grossly underdeveloped special population. This would require legislation. In view of the unemployability of black youth and the deteriorating economic condition of the black and vis-à-vis other minorities, such legislation should not be difficult to enact. In addition, the neglect of institutions with land-grant missions is scandalous, as are the attitudes of the State and Agricultural Departments. Denial will not alter the facts. Additionally, the Title III effort, which under congressional pressure is shifting its emphasis from black to hard-strapped traditionally white institutions, no longer represents viable legislation for the enhancement of the black institutions, as was the original intent. Finally, a great deal of talk took place over the last decade regarding career education. The federal government did little, however, to engage the historically black institutions in the career education movement. At this point in time, with over 50 percent of black youth unemployed against 15 percent of white youth, Kenneth Hoyt's observation that career education for minority and low-income persons was a matter of over-promise and under-delivery represents a gross understatement.[5]

Two brief statements have been made here, hopefully with some sense of interconnection. The first had to do with deficits among black professional workers, with special emphasis on health professionals, life scientists and engineers. Lack of access to schools that train professionals in these areas was alluded to and the point made that the missions and purposes of historically black public institutions have been kept such that they seldom become producers of high level manpower in critical areas. The second statement suggests a planning methodology without going into its minutiae by which the historically black institutions might be validated by the larger society and enabled to assume broader and more realistic missions and purposes. Model building was not attempted, since each situation will be colored by its own unique biases and special interests. Identification of users in each instance, including their needs and interests and current gaps were recommended as a starting point in all cases. This was suggested as a task for an outside consulting agency, prior to the engagement of local citizens' groups in a cooperative planning process. Finally, an attempt was made to place federal roles and

5. Howard, Morgan, the University of the District of Columbia, Coppin and Bowie are located within the Baltimore/Washington corridor. These institutions service in excess of 30,000 students.

responsibilities in the enhancement process into perspective. Local duties and responsibilities were highlighted, leading to state intervention in the matter of supplying most of the needed resources. Federal government intervention at the legal level was duly noted, and reference was made to potential areas of future federal input. Remarks made are not exhaustive, nor are they likely to lead to solutions of the problem described. Such was not intended. Rather, these statements were designed to add to existing interpretations of the problem and to provide a basis for further discussion of it, leading hopefully to more viable solutions than those yet found. Only to the extent interpretation given here of black higher education reality is useful as further discussion and productive action should it be considered as worthwhile.

The State of Maryland was not forgotten as our discussion progressed. Rather, the state's situation was generalized. Baltimore, incidentially, is as good a place as any in which to experiment with the cooperative planning process. Baltimore is also a likely place, along with Washington, D.C., for the federal government to demonstrate its interest in historically black institutions in ways leading to their measurable enhancement, since a good 15 percent of all students left in black institutions can be found within a 40-mile radius of the seat of government.

ADDENDUM I

Enterprising industries would do well to engage in the transferring of technology to blacks so as to assist them to keep pace with Third World Nationals, large numbers of whom are engaged in scientific studies and technology assimilation in the country's principal higher education institutions. Technological transfer should have taken place in the early 20th Century, when so-called industrial education was being promoted by northern philanthropists working in concert with southern-based educators. Hampton and Tuskegee Institutes are prime examples of higher education institutions based on the industrial education concept. Students at these institutions were not sufficiently introduced to the principal branches of production, to the design assemblage and operation of heavy machinery, nor were appropriate on-the-job experiences available at the time. Work in high technology might be added to work with heavy machinery, but one should have another go at industrial education undergirded by a strong liberal arts orientation.

So that the subject discussed here can be projected into the realm of feasibility studies, a Human Resource Development Center with an interdisciplinary staff is recommended. Such a Center should be relatively free standing but lodged at one of the universities. In fact, discussions with the Chancellor of one of the North Carolina institutions have been held with a view toward the writing of a proposal that might result in the design and implementation of such a Center. In any event, a mechanism is suggested through which discussions leading to action approaches to the problem of developing underserviced and underproductive human populations. This is as good a note as any on which to pause and give reflection.

ADDENDUM II

DEVELOPMENTAL EDUCATION: A SPECIAL RESPONSIBILITY FOR INSTITUTIONS SERVICING LARGE NUMBERS OF STUDENTS UNDERSERVICED BY THE SECONDARY SCHOOL SYSTEM

The vast majority of students from lower socio-economic circumstances, among whom black students are disproportionately represented (as many as 90 percent in southern-based public institutions) are in need of developmental education. We know this is not simply because they perform poorly on academic achievement tests such as the SAT and ACT batteries, for these tests are unrelated to innate ability or academic potential. Rather, we know this, because most students from lower socioeconomic circumstances seldom have the benefit of college preparatory backgrounds. That is, most have not studied two natural sciences (or even one). Most have not had two years of algebra, at least one of geometry, one of trigonometry, nor exposure to set theory, elementary probability, precalculus or calculus. Most have not had special English literature courses nor had their reading comprehension skills developed to the point where they score at 12th grade levels or above on reading achievement tests. In short, most are not college ready.

The freshman and lower sophomore years are critical for underserviced students, and particularly students who attend the historically black colleges or are admitted into equal educational opportunity programs at prestigious colleges and universities.

The first three college semesters or quarters, whatever the case may be, represent the last opportunity that underserviced students will have to develop the verbal, quantitative, and science process skills required of persons who will be able to compete favorably for graduate and professional school slots and for professional opportunities in fields associated with a technocratic and post-industrial society. Graduation from college, incidentally, is not necessarily related to appropriate knowledge and skill development. All of this is to say that quality education at the historically black institutions *in particular* is inextricably tied into the capacity of these institutions to fill in critical information and cognitive gaps, and to meet student counseling and general orientation needs.

Developmental education may be defined as teaching appropriate to upgrading achievement outcomes. Let us be specific. Where verbal skills are concerned, students must be able to comprehend at 12th grade levels or above as measured by a standardized reading achievement test, interpret charts and graphs, analyze general situations described in narrative form, organize ideas logically and place them in written form that is relatively free of grammatical and punctuation and sentence structure errors. Where mathematics is concerned, students must be able to solve word problems in which arithmetical or algebraic reasoning is required, manipulate fractions and decimals, conduct algebraic operations involving the solution of simultaneous equations, factor and divide polynomials, solve quadratic equations, graph equations, and apply logarithmic principles. Students should also be familiar with relationships involving circles and their properties, parallel lines and polygons, with trigonometric principles and the pythagorean theorem, set theory, bases of numbers and probability. The verbal and mathematical skills described here can be acquired by students with academic potential, good innate intelligence and reasonable motivation over a 3-semester period at most, given a properly trained education division that interfaces with a structured developmental education program endorsed by and financially supported by the institution and its governing board.

Standard classroom approaches, no matter how attractive, will not work with students in need of developmental education. Self-paced materials offered in modular form must be developed. Classroom lectures must be minimized and individual effort promoted. Focus must be placed on particular topics, which might be drilled or discussed at the small group or individual student level. Student progress must be measured continually and at regular time intervals. Faculty and graduate student assistants providing instruction must be trained and perhaps philosophically re-oriented. All of this must be proceeded by the use of achievement tests for diagnostic, and prescriptive and placement purposes and as a basis for materials development. Developmental education poses difficult and persistent problems, and it is expensive. Developmental education is, nevertheless, unavoidable, if students with special needs are to be treated justly and humanely.

The greatest need, when an institution decides to be serious about servicing developmental education students properly, is for reading instructors. Students scoring below the 25th percentile on a reading test should be required to participate in formal remedial reading programs at the same time that their English usage skills are being upgraded. Several hours of individualized instruction is needed on a weekly basis, using whatever methods and resources are best, based upon each student's reading profile. Students might test out at the 35th percentile or higher, using a post test. A graduate program in which reading specialists are prepared, or graduate assistantships in which providing tutorial services represents the students job assignment, will work well in connection with the developmental program. The same might be said of graduate programs in mathematics and English.

Developmental studies programs should be organized carefully, with the responsibility of each actor spelled out. Each course should be presented to the academic vice president for approval, and later to the faculty senate or its equivalent and to the governing board for approval. Placement decisions should be spelled out, exit criteria detailed and each course spelled out in detail. Monitoring and assessment procedures should be articulated before approval is given. Inconvenience ought never be a factor.

It is not true that historically black institutions are better equipped to provide developmental services or that they are more prone to do so. Efforts in this regard have been carefully examined for the states of Louisiana, Mississippi, and the District of Columbia. More than 100 programs have been looked at, and no indication has been found that historically white institutions, once committed to the developmental education concept, are less adept at mounting successful programs than black institutions. In fact, there is increasing evidence that mainstream institutions are engaging in developmental education with more than a little pride, since such programs afford design, planning and research challenges for enterprising and creative faculty members. This is as it should be, since more whites are in need of developmental education than blacks, although blacks have the greatest need in terms of their disproportionate representation among under-serviced students.